To the family of 985 –
Melissa, Kate and Max

The Blue Leash

A year of mourning

SCOTT D. DOVALE

First published in 2022 by Kuma Bear Publishing

Text copyright © Scott D. DoVale, 2022
Scott DoVale has asserted his moral rights to be identified as the author of this work.

Design and typography copyright © Scott D. DoVale, 2022

This work is copyright, and all rights are reserved. Apart from any use permitted under copyright legislation, no part may be reproduced or transmitted in any form or by any means, nor may any other exclusive right be exercised, without the publisher's prior permission in writing. We welcome your support of the author's rights, so please only buy authorised editions.

ISBN 979-8-986-7768-0-4

Cover and Internal Design: Elysia Clapin
Cover Photograph: Kate DoVale
Illustrations: Amy Wang

Table of Contents

Book I: The Walk	**7**
Where Do I Start . . .	9
The Legend of Kuma	19
The Reality of Finding a Prince	37
The Walk	55
The Dream	71
Journal #1	73
Book II: The Unexpected Path	**105**
An Apple Falls	107
10 Things I Miss	111
A Rise to Prominence	113
The Sounds of Shiba Silence	127
The Blue Leash	145
The Prince	157
Journal #2	159
Book III: The Shadowlands	**187**
125 Steps: A Trilogy	189
10 Things I Regret	207
The Presence of Absence	209
Journal #3	219
Rolling Stone Interview	249
December 14, 2020	271
Acknowledgments	278
About the Author	279

"For a second you see, and seeing the secret, you are the secret. For a second there is meaning! Then the hand lets the veil fall and you are alone, lost in the fog again, and you stumble on towards nowhere for no good reason."
- O'Neill, *Long Day's Journey into Night*

The Blue Leash

Preface

Similar to visual art, mourning lives as an external expression, a visceral response of one's thoughts and emotions, steeped in tradition but inspired, hopefully authentic and infused with a thematic variation of mankind's beauty and frailty. Displaying grief may be judged, admired, copied or criticized. It might inspire some to share and others to mock. But what happens when there is no accepted venue for the artist to show his work, or for the mourner to share his pain? Does it process like Hughes' "dream deferred"? Does it "dry up / like a raisin in the sun? / Or fester like a sore"... or does it just "explode?"

As each year goes by faster and faster, as I keep getting older and older, death has taken a prominent role in my life, occurring more frequently among my family, friends, and co-workers. It always comes unexpectedly, even when it's expected, and takes over my thoughts, my plans, and diminishes whatever I was doing to its bare insignificance. Once it passes its residual effect lingers long after my aged ideals of love, happiness, and peace have left the building.

In the past few years, I have lost significant people in my life without ever thinking to mourn their loss through writing. I witnessed my loving, 82-year-old mother, wither to cancer every day in the last six months of her life, enduring the slow degradation and erosion of her body and mind. Yet, when she died, I never considered writing a sentence or elegy beyond her funeral. Being an aspiring writer for over thirty years, I now find that odd but not unprecedented. My dear father, a spirit of life and laughter, died four months later, as Alzheimer's took him with a ruthless brevity and still not an ode or sonnet. Not an inkling of pen to paper when one of my dearest friends was brutally murdered in Belize, or when my uncle hanged himself in a gas station garage, fifteen minutes after I closed up for the night. More recently, to not render a word bearing my grief and heartbreak when Claire, another beloved friend, passed away this year after a spirited tug-of-war with cancer. And yet? I never touched my keyboard to write a personal reflection, tribute, or condolence letter to the family. Not the slightest inclination to ever pause, reflect, compose or share the critical moments and lessons from those who inspired me and nurtured me throughout my life. Never.

Until now.

I'm writing about Kuma, my dog.

Although my early years were blessed with two loving dogs, their significance in my life was minimal. Missy, a purebred boxer, became our family dog on Christmas Eve, 1964. She burst into our home like a whirling dervish, sniffing every room, licking everyone's face, becoming the new entertainment in the house, like an animated toy, only better. I loved her, but I never walked her, never fed her, never groomed her. I wasn't old enough to see beyond reading Marvel comic books and riding my purple Sting-Ray bike to appreciate the love and joy Missy wanted to share. Years later, as she was suffering from arthritis, my father told me one day how she got loose, ran into the woods, and he couldn't find her anywhere. I swear he told me that, and I swear I believed him.

My second dog was not my dog. He belonged to my uncle who kept him at his gas station, where I worked with my best friend, Nicky. During our last years of high school, we more or less adopted Bruno, a black Belgium Shepherd. Whenever I drove onto the lot for work, he would crash open the front door and race to my car to greet me. During shifts of pumping gas and checking oil, Bruno listened intently to our high school problems and family dysfunctions. My most endearing memory, though, is whenever a customer's car ran over the signal bell hose, while I went out to pump the gas, Bruno would sit in my chair and watch me like a personal bodyguard until I safely returned. This was the first time I ever fell in love with a dog.

Months after starting my first year of college, Nicky called me one night, telling me Bruno got hit by a car exiting the station. My uncle buried him that night below the gas company's illuminated sign. My only instinct was to write Bruno a two-page letter of gratitude, seal it in an envelope, drive the 70 miles to Connecticut to dig up his grave and place the letter next to his body. Back at campus, around 1 am, I received a call from friends who were "stranded" at a bar about a mile away. I picked them up but decided to speed back to campus at 110 MPH, which resulted in totaling my car against a telephone pole. No one was injured but me. And that was from losing Bruno.

This becomes my prelude, my exposition, my character analysis foreshadowing my deep relationship with Kuma and my current, compulsive need to write about him every day. Maybe it was the time of year when he died, or my age making me more susceptible to my emotions. Anxiety before retirement? Mid-life crisis? Maybe his passing was a tectonic shift unearthing my suppressed angers and regrets. All I know is losing Kuma struck me like a Mike Tyson jab, leaving me exposed and hobbled.

The Blue Leash

My only theory concludes that aside from my family, my relationship with Kuma rivaled, and quite often surpassed, most of my human relationships.

It's not that I'm a misanthrope or value people less than Kuma; I've had many solid, healthy relationships, but people are complicated. And unreliable. And self-serving. And often quite contrary. We are constantly shifting our inner lives, revising our beliefs, our values, opinions, alliances, personal desires and sensibilities, constantly growing, adjusting and adapting to a temporal world in a state of never-ending flux. Whereas Kuma provided me with a stable relationship, a reciprocal friendship. He never boasted about himself, never ignored me for a week, never talked behind my back. He was always present, concerned and offered a deep bond, an unwavering loyalty, and a selfless love his entire life. A bond rarely replicated between two human beings.

The influence of Kuma's life deserves more than an anecdote before walking into the woods, never to be seen again. Neither can the impact of his death be captured in a two-page epistle in his shallow grave. *The Blue Leash* stands as a tribute to his life and a yearlong grieving of his death, captured through multiple genres of storytelling inspired by his spirit. Kuma Bear gave me a master class in living; I just didn't know it until I wrote this book.

BOOK I:
The Walk

"A story has no beginning or end: arbitrarily one chooses that moment of experience from which to look back or from which to look ahead."

— Graham Greene

The Blue Leash

Where Do I Start?

Waking up to the local sparrows outside my bedroom window, I'm called to live another original day. Inhaling inspiration from my first cup of Sumatra, I sit delighted by a bowl of fresh blueberries and Greek yogurt, devoting my morning hour to the *LA Times* and a few thoughtful pages from an early Murakami novel. Breathing in the stillness and the silence. Mildly engaged in a few minutes of morning conversation with Melissa, my wife. I soon stand on the porch and wave to her Lexus heading to work before receding back into the house to exercise, clean the kitchen, take a hot shower, and do whatever I wish to do until night.

Another day in the life of being retired. No one telling me to be at school by 7:45. No more faculty meetings, parent meetings, or clubs to monitor. No papers to grade, quizzes to create. No lesson plans to prep. After fifty years of exchanging 40-75 hours a week of my life for a check, many of those good, fruitful years with very few regrets, my servitude to exchanging time for money has come to an end. The career stands complete, the nest is empty, and solitude reigns. Full stop! Actually, guilt and anxiety reign! When Joplin belted out, "Freedom's just another word for nothing else to lose," it was only a great song hook until now. Yes, retirement gave me back my personal freedom to do whatever I want whenever I want, but it's also like sitting under the sword of Damocles. Maybe it's existential dread, or parental DNA, but for some damn reason I keep thinking I should still be working.

Growing up in the 1960s, in a small town in Connecticut, work was ingrained in me as a standard of personal worth: "If you work, you're a good guy; if you don't, you're a bum." My hardworking, Portuguese parents believed in the Puritan work ethic. My Dad managed several jobs, working in construction, real estate, and insurance, while Mom juggled being a telephone operator, secretary, and full-time mother. When I was eight years old, they had me open up a savings account to put my earnings in from mowing lawns, shoveling snow, washing cars, raking leaves, and year-round paper routes. Saving for my future. At nine, when my parents announced their divorce, I immediately started pacing back and forth, back and forth, grasping my worst fear and repeating aloud, "I have to get a job. I have to get a job." I imagined if my parents, the sole keepers of my existence, were able to just leave, then how could I trust anyone else with my life? There is no Santa Claus; there is no God. The future is here. I'M ON MY OWN!

This was the beginning of my journey.

In sixth grade, I decided on my future career. I was standing in the school hallway, leaning against the painted cinder blocks with a hall pass, when I paused to consider what job would suit me best. The first question I posed to myself was "Do I want to work with my head or my hands?" I chose my hands because I wanted to save my brain for myself. I knew I didn't want to wear a suit or tie; I didn't want to work in an office. I wanted to work with people, be creative, have a chance to move up "the ladder" and possibly travel. Within minutes, I thought of being a chef. It fit all my criteria and made perfect sense because people have to eat so I would always have a job. I never thought about it again.

After graduating from the CIA (Culinary Institute of America) in 1976, I worked in kitchens for the next 24 years - line cook, sous chef, chef, executive chef. From hotels and fine dining to bistros and country clubs. From New York and Atlanta to Lake Tahoe, San Francisco and Los Angeles. A life equally populated by Anthony Bourdains and Chef Ramsays, the food service industry offered everything my sixth-grade self was looking for, including one aspect I didn't see coming - it demanded my time, commitment and loyalty. It wasn't until my daughter's birth in 1996 when I recognized the culinary life was for the young and single, not a profession conducive to raising a family. Actually, it was on Father's Day, after working fifteen grueling hours, when my wife and I decided that one of us needed to make a change. I gladly gave up my executive chef job at a country club, returned to college for an English degree and became a high school teacher. I always loved to read, write, and talk about literature, and I thought having summer's off with the kids would be great, so why not? Oh my God! I thought you only worked to make money, pay bills and support a family. I never knew you could actually love your job!

Teaching was my calling; I just didn't get the message until I was forty. This new world of education presented me with a purposeful, enjoyable, heartwarming lovefest of literature, analytical discussions, personal conversations, and an all-consuming, rejuvenating lifestyle. Every year I turned my parochial school classroom into an art installation, filling it with seasonally dressed mannequins, urban wall murals, posters of Emerson, Kerouac and Walter White, 360 degrees of ceiling Christmas lights, and classic rock/rap/pop/techno music during every break, lunch and vocabulary quiz. The atmosphere offered the students a haven, a safe place to share their thoughts and lives in essays, journals and discussions. It offered me even more. I WAS ON FIRE! For the first 10-15 years, I taught with enough energy to light up the school and left with even more. My years of teaching were as close to finding my purpose as any human being could possibly hope for in their lifetime.

However, as I approached the last few years, after grading at least 330 essays, 330 tests, and innumerable quizzes each semester, my energy was no longer being replenished. The joy and elan was replaced by weariness; the routine more furrowed than Thoreau's path from his hut to the pond. Although *The Scarlet Letter* and *The Great Gatsby* still warmed my soul, and still gave me license to tell kids to be true to themselves and yes, we are all held back by the past, my life outside of the classroom became more indentured to the progressive whims of academia. Each year my beloved vocation demanded more - more meetings, more emails, and more well-intentioned but misguided influences - and I ended up having much less.

I planned on retiring to shed the "faded wardrobe" of the past and reclaim my inner life, strongly believing a third act was still possible. That belief was fostered by two things – it would give me time to write and more time to spend with Kuma. As an unpublished writer of short stories and plays, and receiving a modicum of praise from respected voices, I still believed in my voice to write something of value. As a lover of my eleven-year-old dog, I could be more present in walking him, playing with him, lunching with him, and having a beer with him while writing the next, semi-great American novel. Pasadena would be our oyster and chew bone! But what I intended life to be and what it turned out to be, well, in the prophetic words of Robert Burns' poem: "... the best-laid schemes o mice an' men" go often awry." What happened was Kuma died.

On December 14, 2019, the importance of retiring dissipated, felt more meaningless, lonelier, and did I really want to be by myself every day? In many ways, as Kuma and I were getting older, retirement had become more about us. My kids had left for college and my wife still had five more years of work, so I believed this would be our time to grow even closer. Even if we were slowing down, our days could be spent together on the porch, at the beach, in the den. I'd be able to cook fresh food for his meals, maybe have a playdate or two, walk a little, nap a little. Together. I admit at my age naivety is not an attractive quality, or an excuse for anything, but I never, never, never considered for one second he wouldn't be with me, so his death left me with many questions: Why did he die so soon? What do I do without him? How can my life be normal without this surly recluse, this independent soul who loved me so much? And why did he love me so much? And why did he nip so many people's ankles?

When we adopted Kuma at eight weeks old, he was small, but his behaviors were quite large. Mature? Wunderkind-ish? He didn't seem like a "normal" dog. An ingratiating, over-loving, rambunctious, run-amok, licking machine kind of dog, he was not. Most nights he would sit in the den, imposing himself on the communal psyche while the family read or watched TV, sending telepathic questions in my direction with his eyes, patiently waiting for clarifying answers. Whenever I fed him, he'd watch from a distance, feigning interest, possibly judging my technique, or simply waiting for me to walk away. It puzzled me to no end. I remember seeing his supine Superman stretch on the kitchen floor for the first time, and I asked him, "Where did you come from?' "Why are you here?" and "Are you a human masquerading as a fox?" He disarmed my wisdom, my age, and dismantled all my preconceived notions of a dog. And then it came to me – maybe he's an AI prototype planted by the government, or maybe he was sent by Amazon to listen to our commercial needs, a more endearing version of Alexa. Or maybe he was sent to me by God.

In writing about his life, I needed to research the beginning of his journey. To understand his instincts, his predilections, his habit of licking his inner thighs until they were hairless. Much of who we are is hidden and unknown to others as we get older. *Why did Kuma, who never paid attention to Grandma, curl up on her medical bed everyday as she was dying?* As our lives progress, as we move to new careers, relationships and locations, the history of our personal evolution dissolves as new people come into our lives. Since I left my childhood home in Connecticut, no one ever knew what drove me so hard.

Why is Kuma more sentinel than participant? No one understood why I never trusted anyone who showed interest in me. *What happened to his parents?* Only those who knew me from the beginning. Who knew my parents, my brother, my family. Who knew me in 2nd grade when I ate dirt to impress girls, or played with Matchbox trucks for hours in the yard until dusk. *Why did he nab cat poop from the litter box like he was poaching a chicken from a hen house?* As much as I lack the current fervor for Ancestry.com and such, I do understand the value. We spend our lives searching for who we are and some of those answers can be found by those who came before us, who influenced us genetically. *And how did Kuma become an emotional rock for all of us? In our rejoices and our failures, in our wins and our losses, in all things family?* I became intrigued by where Kuma was born, who his parents were, and what my dear puppy went through to find me. *How in God's name did he find me?* Having lost touch with Kuma's breeder, I analyzed his behaviors, characteristics, and proclivities, briefly referred to his astrological sign, Gemini, and his Myers-Briggs results (ISFP-A / introverted, sensing, feeling, perceiving-assertive), in order to write his origin story.

Yet, after all my observations and data, something was missing. My synthesis and conjectures did not result in a birth worthy of Kuma's steadfast loyalty, innate compassion, wisdom, and intuitive sense of meeting every moment. Kuma's origin demanded I incorporate his spiritual nature and the historical roots of his ancestors. Something to definitely explain not only his physical but his metaphysical. More like a fusion of a Biblical messiah, a shaman, and Joseph Campbell's "hero" on a quest, intertwining the natural with the supernatural.

Finally, all these concepts opened the pathway for me to interpret his extraordinary demeanor, his source of inspiration, and why this princely canine's death affected me so much. But to help me remember, to rekindle his spirit, to live in the present as I created his fictional past, I knew one thing - I needed to start at the beginning.

"The beginning is the most important part of the work."
— Plato, *The Republic*

"And above all, watch with glittering eyes the whole world around you because the greatest secrets are always hidden in the most unlikely places. Those who don't believe in magic will never find it."
— **Roald Dahl**

The Legend of Kuma Bear: The Origin Story

I. The Creation of the Shiba Inu

The boys and girls pawed one another, struggling for a front row seat. Their mother nuzzled them to be still and pay attention. One of them sat in the back, aware this might be the last time his father, Sky, told them a story. Sky waited for silence and then began.

"Myths are forged from symbolic steel. Alchemy formed from figurative elements as strong and unwavering as any words ever written by human kind. Cultures bear the moral weight of these ancestral tales, retold to them from generation to generation. Most of these stories weave the natural with the supernatural, guiding their people to a transcendent life beyond their earthly woes, while a few merely change the course of their culture's history. That is our story today."

Sky scratched his ear and shook his neck back and forth, as his collar tightened, his tags clanged and the room's temperature rose. He suddenly felt the weight of the moment, looking over to his wife for a bit of extra fortitude, both of them knowing how bittersweet this story ends.

"Many centuries ago, two of the greatest gods, Izanagi and Izanami, were called upon by their almighty father, Saisho, to come to Earth and oversee his creation. Guided by ancestral wisdom, they soon developed a superior culture, one to lead all earth's inhabitants to fulfill their own *Reiteki unmei*, their own spiritual destinies. Through this divine blue print, Japan's islands were formed and populated with one of the greatest, most resilient, civilizations in human history.

However, as the chronicles of the past have witnessed, people lose their way. Drawn to earthly pleasures and selfish desires, humans tend to abandon their souls. King Achebe, a noted wiseman, once cautioned if ever that should happen in any tribe, 'Things fall apart; the centre cannot hold.' Thus, all civilizations will eventually contribute to their own demise. And so, after witnessing Japan's repudiation of their own sacred fortune, Saisho decided to break his Golden Bond to his children. He believed interfering with his offsprings' creation would be justified if he created a different species, one solely capable of saving the Japanese culture.

Saisho designed the Chîsana Kamis, the 'little gods,' with an unbreakable will to stay true to their *kokoro* – their heart, mind, and soul. Their presence exuding confidence and nobility, while carrying an internal shield of spiritual strength and independence, strong enough to protect their assignments from Susano-o, the god of mischief. Most importantly, Chîsana Kamis' would be granted unparalleled fealty to serve their assignments with honor their entire lives. Their primary purpose? To enlighten their human to see life as a spiritual journey, not a destination; to show how the world was a magical sphere to inspire and serve, not a pedestrian arena to achieve and compete. In creating these guardians, though, Saisho recognized one major obstacle - how to integrate the Chîsana Kamis into the world without undermining the hearts and minds of the people. And so, after gathering with the gods of the suns, the earth, the sky and the moon, Saisho molded their perfect form - he created the Shiba Inu."

Sky paused. He surveyed the room. There was silence. Five little mouths were agape hungrily waiting for his next words. One of the twins had fallen asleep. Sky continued.

"The Shiba Inu originated from the rib of the mighty Akita, powerful dogs and conquerors of the mountainous Northern region of Odate, Japan. From their inception, Akitas were destined to physically lead men and to protect them from threatening wildlife. Using their enormous chests as shields, and their sharp, powerful teeth to quake any foreign beast, Akitas were recognized throughout Japan for what Saisho intended them to be: fearless warriors. Unfortunately, Shibas had to tread a more difficult path.

In the small village of Dakung, home of the largest Shiba Inu population, lived the Nokus, poorly educated farmers, whose main concern was survival, not spiritual awakening. Influenced by the Shiba's diminutive size and high-pitched yodel, the Nokus raised them all to be 'warriors of the bush,' hunting small game and cultivating land. Yet, even though their divine purpose was diminished for many, many years, the Shiba Inus never gave up hope.

Our forefathers understood that the Nokus' failure to recognize the Shiba's potential reflected how humans constantly impeded their own enlightenment. Forests were decimated rather than revered. The blue skies polluted and vast oceans enslaved. Rather than seeing these life sources as stepping stones for man's awakening, even the natural world was sadly deprived of its highest potential. For many, many years our ancestors patiently prayed to Saisho to send a savior to help us fulfill our destiny, but it would take many generations for their prayers to be answered. But they were answered."

II. A Moment of Reckoning

"By 1600 AD, after centuries of wars, famines, and hard labor, the Shiba Inu began to shed its foraging role and reclaim its divine birthright. The first sect of Shiba, the Kanazawa Shiba Inu, escaped the rural Japanese culture by fleeing to the Kumakura mountains, where they lived among the Samarai in the late 17th century. Living among each other, the warriors soon discerned the Shiba's solitary nature and divinity, giving them a place of honor inside the warrior's home and never assigning them to hard labor again. In return, the Shibas taught the Samarai the bushido, the "way of the warrior," instilling them with loyalty, honor, and service to man, transforming the warriors into a passionate community of peacemakers. However, the rest of the Japanese culture remained oppressive, minimizing the Shiba's potential and seeing them as nothing more than 3/5 of an Akita.

The Blue Leash

It was not until Kithune 'Kit' Shinshinja sacrificed his life when the destiny of the Shiba Inu changed forever. During World War II, Kit's assignment, Colonel Yamanoto, became instrumental to the Imperial Japanese Navy by encrypting communications. By two years old, Kit's attempts to sway the Colonel's allegiance from the war repeatedly failed. Despite dropping a tennis ball at his feet every day and standing at the Colonel's desk with his leash in his mouth every night, the Colonel remained steadfast. So, in the middle of everyone's dreams, Kit deserted the Colonel, leaving his innate loyalty behind. This treasonous act soon caused his family severe shame and embarrassment, but Kit believed in his destiny. He never saw them or talked to them again.

Sky paused. He stared at his first litter, the best pups in the whole world, knowing this would be their last night together. If only they could stay young. Sky remembered hearing this story the last day he saw his father. Life goes by so fast. The huddled little masses of fur grew impatient, squeaking their yodels for more.

Walking miles away from everything known to the mysterious white sands of Shirahama Beach, Kit dropped down wanting nothing more than sleep. Several minutes passed before the palm fronds woke to sway Kit's attention east, and the warm breeze prodded him to the edge of the crashing waves. He anchored himself before the blue abyss trembling in isolation, searching the horizon for the missing piece to his life. Looking up, he howled, 'Is this why I was born? To fail my assignment? To shame my family? I am so much more. Please, help me!'

Suddenly, an impenetrable darkness draped the sky, as the wind flexed, the thunder clapped, and the biting salt air unified them to ambush Kit's growing fears. His mind sank into the depths of the ocean, the power of the elements, and the insignificance of his life on Earth. Choosing the only honorable path, he climbed to the farthest cliff overlooking the water. The weight of Kit's shame lowered his paws onto the damp rocks, to the very end of the earth. His only thought before his final step was to ask Saisho's forgiveness for his failure as a Chîsana Kami. But Kit's thoughts – "

"Dad?"

"Shh! Dilly!"

"But Dad? This is really sad."

"Dilly! Sit. This is important."

Sky stared at Bear, his oldest son, who remained in the back, absorbing every word as gospel.

"But Kit's thoughts were cut short by the red moon's flickering light on the waves, offering his eyes a radiant path from the threatening waters to the glistening rock in the distance. Squinting through the mist, Kit discovered the silhouette of the sacred red Torii, the Shinto gateway to the spiritual world. The mythical Torii stood 40 feet high and 100 yards away, with nothing but thrashing waves and jagged rocks below and between. Kit believed this was his only chance for redemption. If he could find a way to pass through the gate, if he could transition to the other world, he might be given a second chance to fulfill his purpose.

The sky softened. The threatening storm took its orders to hold still and the red moon beamed down upon Kit. And so he jumped! Some Shibas believe Susano-o pushed Kit into the ocean, thinking he would surrender to fear and uncertainty, but it doesn't matter. His will to live, his belief in his life's purpose was too great. At that very moment, Kit saved our breed and brought us to freedom."

III. The Legend Begins

"Immediately submerged in darkness, a sharp panic brushed Kit's fur, plunging him deeper and deeper into the abyss. Rapidly sinking, he centered himself, his mind and his spirit, and began paddling his fours until he found himself face-to-face with a furry, glowing seashell. A seashell, unlike anything creation itself had ever seen clinging to the rocks. Spun in a cornucopian wave of exoskeletons, the neocancilla takiisaoi absorbed the moon's light, revealing a thick, plush coat of red sesame fur encompassing the spiral shell. And then her fur began to glow. Kit's shock spewed out a full-throated yodel underwater, but the seashell remained still.

'Kit?'

The shell blinked.

'Kit?'

Kit's eyes grew wide. The voice was speaking to him! A smile rose on his face like he was home, like his mom and dad were hugging him endlessly. He felt a natural connection with the shell, with the water, with life itself, sensing his dishonor and shame were not forever. The seashell hummed and smiled back. His instinct to risk his life saved his life. The shell began to unravel as a brilliant, white light emanated from its center. His purposeful life. The shell's light drew Kit closer until he willingly entered into her expanding, conical folds. The shell twisted tight once again. Kit barely wound his tail inside before surrendering his furry muzzle and weary body to sleep. As

The Blue Leash

soon as the seashell was sealed, she began rotating, faster and faster, creating a vortex, expanding until the radiant conch morphed into a giant hawksbill turtle. Slow in motion but quick in heart, Harriet lifted her neck scanning for danger as she began her descent, paddling away from Kit's life of hopeless servitude to a new world, far away from his internal darkness to a brilliant light of hope."

Sky was forced to stop as the excitement rose. The huddled little masses of fur grew impatient, squeaking their yodels of questions and wonder.

"And then what?"

"I want to go inside a shell!"

"What's a shell?"

From the back, Bear prompted his father. "Dad, the seashell turned into a turtle?"

"Yes! The seashell was an ôbake, a shapeshifter. Guided by Neptune and Suijin, she swam for forty days and forty nights before bringing Kithune to the shores of Coos Bay."

"That's where we live, isn't it?" Sun and Moon questioned.

"That's right! And this is where Kithune started our great community, fathering more than fifty Shibas. Saisho had sent us our savior."

"But who was the mother?" Dally asked.

Sky barked. "Well, let me finish! Once Harriet released Kit from her shell, she explained how a week before she saved Kit, she dreamt a great war would soon destroy much of the Shiba world. A woman in the dream told her the Chosen One would appear at Shirahama Beach on the night of the red moon to save the Shiba breed. Harriet woke up knowing her ikigai, her "reason for being," was to find Him and carry Him to safety. Then as she smiled at Kit, she spun around three times, transforming herself into the most beautiful Shiba ever, turning into your 12X great grandmother, Madame Dame. At the same time, Ms. Northstar, a breeder and human prophet of Shibas, walked down from her shoreline ranch and introduced herself to Kit and Madame, welcoming them to live on her farm. Madame recognized Ms. Northstar as the woman in her dream. She gave our ancestors time to grow and strengthen their community back to a purposeful era for all Shibas. Now we wait for the Transitional One, the one chosen to lead us forward to our truthful place on Earth. And from that moment, Madame Dame beget Marume, who beget Beni Hana, who beget Skywalker, who then sired your dear father, Sky."

Wild applause and yodels.

"Wow! Dad, you're like a king!"

"Dad, that was the best story ever!"

Sky bowed his head, "Thank you."

Akane stood next to Sky, proudly pointing her ears, softly shedding a tear. Sky's words rekindled her father's regal tone when he taught her and her siblings the Shiba history. Her spirit knew well that Sky was nervous to pronounce the Shiba creed, but he delivered it as soundly as her father did, as her grandfather did. Her children were never more riveted than tonight.

But no one was more riveted than Bear.

What Sky did not tell his pups was how the community had believed he was the Transitional One, bred to be the greatest angel, the *Saidai no tenshi*, on Earth. His physical superiority, his intelligence, composure and unparalleled loyalty to the caged community all pointed to his divinity. Even he thought at one time it might be true, but as happens to the best laid plans, his beautiful wife, Akane, entered into his caged world. Although throwing his spiritual kismet into canine disarray, Sky willingly embraced his path of mortality, letting go of any desire for astral fame and fortune. So end many dreams, as others are divinely begun.

V. Prince Kuma

"Then I met your mother and decided to become the best husband and father I could be and like magic, the greatest litter of all time was born, and their names were Dilly, Dally, Sun, Moon, Blue, and Bear."

"That's me! Dilly!"

"And me! Dally!"

"That's right. And like Kit and Madame Dame, your life's journey will be to find your ikigai. We all question our purpose, and why we are so quickly separated from our families, but we are Shiba Inus. We have withstood centuries of struggles. Here, at home, you are happy and loved, but you will not grow. You will never become the Chisana Kamis you were meant to be. Saisho will place you where your gifts will be needed the most. Remember, we are of spirit, even though people on Earth will only see us as dogs. Domestic creatures. But as your grandfather always says, "All dogs are equal. Then Saisho made the Shiba Inu."

The family nuzzled, growled, and bit each other's neck, sharing their love until time would kidnap their joy. Akane took her children outside to review their favorite games – hide the sock, chase me until you can't, and rip the mail - while Sky prepared himself for the most important speech of his life.

"Bear, stay here for a minute."

Bear was the oldest by a few seconds, so he strove to be the ideal Shiba for his brothers and sisters. He did not listen to a different drummer; he only listened to the retold tales about Saisho's divine plan, the Samarai Shiba Code, and how Shibas were here to honor and serve their assignments. How Kit and Madame Dame courageously traveled to save their breed. He yodeled and prayed to embody all things Shiba, to be like his father, but deep in his heart, he aspired to be even more, to be as great as the greatest Akita of all time – Hachikô.

"Yes, Dad?"

"Did you like the story?"

"That one's my favorite!"

"Good. Kitsune was a divine Shiba. His life reflects courage, independence, and faith. He believed in something greater than himself. He believed in Saisho's creation, to help us be better tomorrow. We live here today because of him, but now we wait for the next great Shiba, the Transitional One, who will guide us to all lands so we may become a positive presence in every human's life. *(Pause)* Many in our community thought that I was the One."

"Really, Dad?"

"But I wasn't. My purpose was to be your dad. *(Pause)* Bear, have you noticed your tail curls more than the others?

"Does it?"

"Or how no one has a red streak down their back like yours? How your fur is thicker than anyone else's in our community?

"No, Dad. Why? Am I ok?"

Sky stopped. How do you tell your son he is the One? How his features bear the historical path of Kit? That his tail curls like Kit's after being in Harriet's shell? How his back was blazoned with the mark of the red moon, or his fur doubled, incarnating Harriet's fur with his own. But why burden his two-month-old son with such a weight? If Bear is truly the One . . . .

"Of course, you're ok. Bear, you are the best of us. A gentle stare that commands attention. A strong *kokoro* that sits confidently in the stillness. A peace found in the breath of life, and a steel will more stubborn than my own."

"That's good! That's what a Shiba should be."

"Right. But you are more than just . . . just be yourself. I'm sure your assignment will need all of your gifts."

"How do you know?"

"Because Saisho would not waste your gifts."

"But how will I know what my assignment will need?"

"Because you are a prince. My Prince. Prince Kuma? Get ready to change the kingdom!"

The following morning, tears and hugs trailed behind Bear and his siblings as they left their parents, riding over seven hundred miles down Interstate 5 to their future homes in Southern California. Aside from Ms. Northstar's luggage, the

The Blue Leash

well-travelled van accommodated six crates with blankets, food, and water. Not quite as treacherous as Kit's journey, Bear had a warm bed, air conditioning and a window seat looking out at the stars to dream ... to dream how Kit might have felt the same nervous excitement watching the world speed by as he left one world for another how the trip was taking forever how they might be lost maybe Ms. Northstar forgot where they were going and then how close he was to meeting his assignment will they get along and everything was going so fast might never see his mom or dad again miss them so much right now want to be home but must be strong but what if he doesn't have a chance to glorify Saisho to be the best Chîsana Kama ever or maybe ... or maybe ... and then Bear fell asleep with uncertainty for the very last time.

"Dogs have a way of finding the people who need them, filling an emptiness we didn't even know we have."
– Thom Jones

The Blue Leash

The Reality of Finding a Prince

July 4, 2008. *(Overheard on a BBQ patio in Pasadena with a beer in hand):*

"I NEVER want a dog! Really, I don't. I'm a cat person. Cats embody the best virtues of a family pet. They're independent, low maintenance. They don't have to be walked all the time. You can leave them for days with food and water. And they're super clean. You don't find fur everywhere. You don't have to clean up their poop. Well, the litter box but . . . but my 12-year-old daughter constantly keeps begging us to get a dog. Nothing's more important to her than a dog. Every time she says, 'We'll feed her and walk her and you'll see, Dad,' I know how that goes, and I have enough stuff in my life. Too much. Working, paying bills, cooking dinner, my wife's to-do list, chauffeuring the kids everywhere – soccer games, karate classes, piano lessons, friends' houses – and then meetings, emails, lesson planning, grading 110 essays three times a semester. I don't have time for a dog. Of course, I'm a teacher so free time is non-existent. That thing about teachers getting weekends off? Right. I barely get any time to relax. But my daughter's been asking for more than six months. Will not let it go! The last time she brought it up I kind of raised my voice a bit too loud: 'We are not getting a dog! You're not going to take care of him! Or her. What about Frasier, Emerson, Ajax, Salem and Boots? Who feeds them now? I do! Who cleans their litter boxes? I do! I don't have time to take care of a dog. Walk him. Play with him. Not to mention the cost. Tons of food, vet bills, medical bills, boarding them during vacations. Can't do it, sweetie. Uh – uh. Sorry. Drop mike. End of conversation.' She can be so persistent but . . . so can I."

When I was seventeen, while high school friends aspired to be doctors, engineers, lawyers and such, my only goal was to be a great dad. Strange, being that my dad divorced my mom when I was nine and split up our family, but he was a great dad, nonetheless, staying in my life, rarely missing a beat. He taught me about life when I needed it most, especially how important it was for a child to have stability. So, here I was living my perfect life – a teaching career, a house, a wife, two children, a few cats. A full life. An ideal existence. Why ruin it with a dog?

The Blue Leash

July 15, 2008. "Dad? It's not just for me. Max wants a dog, too. I just read every boy should have two things – a dog and a father willing to let him have one. And you had a dog when you were a kid, right? Sissy? Or Missy? A man's best friend! Please? Mom said it was OK with her. I SWEAR we will take care of her. I can do this. I mean, we can do this! Tell him, Max!"

Nine-year-old Max. The sweetest, most loving son declared his sibling allegiance.

"I think a dog would be really cool, dad. I'm with Kate."

"Kate, one more time. We have five cats, one over the city limit. Five birthdays. Five cats. And you promised - "

"Dad? I was 6 when we got Frasier! I was 7 when we got Emerson and Ajax. What did you expect? I didn't know cats only sit around and clean themselves. Or scratch you when you pick them up to play. I want a pet I can hug and cuddle.

"Cats can do that. They're as good as dogs. Only better."

She exhales, "They're not the same. Every family needs a dog. V Bae has a dog. Karolyn has a dog. Even Grandma wants one, and she's going to die soon!" As she shuffles her feet and trembles her shoulders, tears and sniffles accompany her down the hallway. With the saddest of touches, she opens her bedroom door and whispers back, "You're very mean. But I love you. Good night, Papa." She softly closes her door, the click of the latch cutting through the hallway's intolerant silence.

Oh, that one hurts every time. What I hate the most about being a dad is having to say no. I wish everything was yes, but it's not. That's not real life and if I'm supposed to teach my kids anything, it's how to be resilient, how to roll with the punches, turn failures into success. To know which battles are worth fighting for and especially, how to take no for an answer.

July 16, 2008. As the final round of the AT&T National was playing on TV, we drove to the Pasadena Humane Society. The kids were sitting in the back, quiet and well-behaved, like any noise might make their dad change his mind. Driving with my natural, passive-aggressive mindset, the car stopped sharply at red lights and took each turn with defeated resignation. We pulled into the overcrowded parking lot scraping my front end, and then back out, parking half a block down the street. I sat in the car for a moment, asking my young, zealous brainwashers for a bit of silence, wondering if this was karmic payback for my twenties or the result of inheriting my dad's weak spine.

Distant barking grew louder as we approached the entrance, and I knew, I swear I could smell this day would change my life forever. Kate straightened her shoulders and checked her puppy-patterned dress before striding in to present her case, unaware the shelter willingly gives you a dog. She had googled "dogs who get along with many cats," finding beagles, golden retrievers, and chihuahuas

The Blue Leash

to be the consensus choices. She created Excel sheets comparing the different breeds, the daily/monthly/annual costs of each small dog and ended with a feeding/walking schedule, leaving me a box to initial each day upon their completion.

"We would like to see the dogs. Do you have any beagles?"

"Yes, we do."

"Great! My brother and I read they are the perfect dog for our fi . . . four cats."

"Was that on Wikipedia? Beagles are scent dogs. Hunting dogs. They chase cats. You might want to see pugs or spaniels. Even chihuahuas. Do you like chihuahuas?"

"Yes, but my dad thinks they're all yappie, weenie dogs."

"But they're very good with cats."

"Dad?"

"Kate, I said I would be open to a beagle. Not a pugsley dog or a weenie dog."

"Shiba Inus are very good with cats. And they're not 'weenie dogs.' You're probably not going to find one in a shelter, but they're very cute. What's a pugsley dog?"

"What's a Shiba Inu?"

Riding back home, Kate sat teary-eyed, red-faced, unleashing a bursting nova of emotions. Her efforts were not being recognized. She and Max would grow up with black holes in their hearts, everybody in the family hates her, and I was a "soul-sucking monster," "a dream killer," and a "terrible dad, the worst ever," who didn't love his kids, and then I wasn't, but I was definitely not being fair. Something like that. My rearview mirror reflected a young girl wrestling with her shattered dreams, but I said nothing.

My silence did not come from my passivity but a shameful smugness arising from fulfilling my duties as a father while still getting a favorable conclusion for myself. Not my best day.

"Kate, this is the universe telling us it's not the right time. If we were meant to have a dog today, we would have hit every green light, found the perfect parking space, and I wouldn't have scraped my car. The staff lady would have shown us the perfect beagle, and she would have already been named . . . what name did you want to give her?"

"Princess."

"Princess! But it didn't work out that way, did it? Let's wait another month or two. Wait for the universe to tell us when it's time. O.K.?"

I remember sighing. It felt like I dodged a bullet, but why? I thought about when we had our kids. When we had Kate, my wife and I could take turns holding her and watching her, giving the other one a break. When we had Max, life felt more restrictive. Two parents, two children. Like adding one more thing would crumble our life like a fallen Jenga tower. Then it hit me. I was afraid of losing control. And I sighed again.

The Blue Leash

Two hours later, as Anthony Kim was putting on the 16th hole to take the lead, Kate summoned me into my office. Sitting in my leather chair, she turned her authority to me, as her brother propped himself up on the chair's back legs, peering over her shoulder with feigned gravitas. They had researched Shiba Inus on the internet and prepared their PowerPoint presentation. Little RBG stood, rapped her hairbrush gavel on my desk and began her prosecution: "Ladies and gentlemen, I will present to you a dog so perfect for our family, you will have no choice but to agree we should have a Shiba Inu. My first pieces of evidence are gathered from expert witnesses from the world of dogs. *(She clicks through her first slides)*. From Dogtime.com: 'The Shiba Inu is a Japanese breed known for a bold, fiery personality.' They are 'interesting, intelligent, and strong-willed.' *Not* a weenie dog. Wikipedia clamors: 'Shibas tend to exhibit an INDEPENDENT nature.' They are 'charming, fearless, faithful, confident. These dogs are *VERY CLEAN*, so grooming needs will likely be minimal.' *The Daily Paws* mentions how they 'walk to the beat of their own drum,' completely satisfied roaming the house without too much attention. Finally, the American Kennel Club says the Shiba is 'very cat-like' in its cleanliness and demeanor. They are 'INDEPENDENT dogs.' To summarize for the jury, Shiba Inus have the same characteristics that my father likes in cats. They are CAT DOGS! Next! I would like to present a witness. Mom? Come in, Mom!"

My wife marches in, the innocent abettor to a patriarchal betrayal, and sits directly in front of my daughter.

"Please tell the court your thoughts about our family getting a Shiba Inu. Remember, you are under oath."

"I think they are very cute. They are exactly the type of dog we need. Very catlike. Independent, clean. Only a little bigger. Even though their fur - "

"Even though their fur is beautiful! That will be all. Thank you, Mom! Let me close with Exhibit B - pictures of Shiba Inus. *(Kate clicks through pictures of Shibas.)* Notice how the puppies have cute bear faces like stuffed animals. These are recent pictures from a breeder in Oregon. In fact, she has ten puppies available to adopt, and she's bringing them down to Los Angeles next week. I called her to make sure. So, ladies and gentleman, after all this evidence, looking at all these pictures, there is only one conclusion you can possibly reach. And if your heart hasn't already grown three sizes, if you don't think we should have a Shiba puppy, then you're not human! I rest my case."

July 23, 2008. Traveling north on the 210 freeway, at ten in the morning, I felt reasonably calm. Winding through a familiar route, listening to classic rock, little traffic, reliving miles and memories from our less-populated years. My anxiety, however, began to elbow my forehead and wrestle away the steering wheel as we headed towards the congested chaos of Interstate 5. Metallic herds vying

The Blue Leash

to cross lanes without signals. Aggressive, phone-between-the-legs drivers brawling to cut in at 80 mph, flashing brake lights, a few screeches of rubber, and . . . we're stuck in bumper-to-bumper traffic. The forty-five minute drive to pick up our new puppy downshifted into a two hour snail-a-thon, giving me plenty of time to repeatedly roll my eyes and ask myself, "What am I doing?"

Don't get me wrong. I was fine. The backseat minions were yelling out names from every movie, TV show, and musical artist they knew to coin the perfect moniker for our newest family member. *Zac, the Weeknd, Swift, Lil Jam, Jay Z, Beyonce, Lil Wayne.* But I was fine. Traveling with my kids, while my wife stayed home to make room at the inn, and a double double In-N-Out cheeseburger and animal fries waiting for me when all this was done. Fine. *Rihanna, Jack Black, Mr. Krabs.* I did pray for a minor earthquake to postpone this adoption but only because my kids were finally branching out more. Volleyball practices. Video games at friend's houses. *Nelly, 50 cent, Juno, Joker.* Pajama parties. Paint ball invitations. *Zack, Cody.* And I was getting more personal time back. Not that I prematurely resented the dog. *Mr. Ed, Kafka, McCandless (mine).* It was just the worst time for the wrong pet in my universe.

"Mom said you would do this. She said you really have a soft heart. We just don't see it."

"Did she?"

"Yeah. She said you would cave if we tried hard enough.

"Yep. I'm the caveman."

After a few detours and a final traffic alert, we arrived at Granite Ridge, home to the breeder's SoCal hosts, the proud owners of three Shiba Inus. Wearing champagne smiles, they led us through their house, featuring a rotunda foyer and travertine tiles, which abruptly morphed into a 1920s storefront concealing activities much more nefarious than bootlegging liquor. The laundry room, den and guest bedroom had been commandeered by their dogs, occupying three large crates, more like domestic stables, with food bowls, water troughs and a surplus of blankets for "the children." Stripped of human furniture, with paw-smudged, sliding glass doors to the backyard, these cells exhibited my worst fears of tumbleweed fur, slimy meat bones and the faint smell of urine.

"Aren't they cute?"

The universe was mocking me.

Keri Northstar, the Oregon breeder, greeted us in the backyard. She was a mid-60s woman, dressed in dirty paw blue jeans, plaid cotton top and a scarved head holding back an unruly band of red hair. As we stood on the patio watching Shiba puppies playing Ringolevio, she extended her hands in their direction, anointing them with her exuberance.

"There're my babies! Eight weeks old. Birthed by my very best. Their ancestors go all the way back to Japan. Very independent, full of life as you can see. Very, very strong-willed. You'll need to make them know you're the Alpha, or else they will be. There are ten – I'm sorry, there are eight of them. Two of them were adopted this morning. A few more families are coming soon, but look around. You can choose one right now if you'd like."

Kate and Max stood agape at the galaxy of puppies orbiting the yard. Running and hopping, leaping and bouncing, rolling, rolling, rolling on the lawn, on the woodchips, no direction, no purpose, moving for the love of moving, for the joy of being free in Whitman's "hopeful green stuff woven," with high-pitched whimpers, melting the most cynical mind with the radiance of innocence like kittens or mini-angels! The kids kept exhaling their "Oohs" and "Ahhs," leading to Kate's animated crescendo, "They're soooo cute!" and ending with Max's existential dilemma, "Dad, which one should we choose?"

"Well, play with them a bit. Take your time, but not too long. Maybe you should choose the one that chooses you, that speaks to your heart. Remember, Kate? Trust the universe."

Bear maintained his erect posture on the edge of the tiled patio. He sniffed the leg of the tall man standing next to him. "Hmmm, that's a strange smell," he thought. His fellow pups were busy running in circles, chasing each other, and playfully biting ears and throats. Bear wanted to join in, but his mission was to supervise and ensure his brothers and sisters were safely chosen. He exhaled his concerns, admiring the dazzling sun, the vast sky, the distant San Gabriel mountains. He listened to the sounds of pleasant jabber, the painless yelps, as his thoughts drifted to his parents. His dad explaining why they had to leave. His mom licking his face and crying. He wished he were home. He looked up at the tall man watching the two young people like his dad always did when their family was together. Serious, but smiling. Bear's thoughts pointed his ears to the noisy yaps from his twin brothers' attention-getting antics. Dilly and Dally were doing flips and prat falls, gathering everyone's attention, everyone except the tall man, who began walking away by himself.

As two more expectant parents arrived and prated with Ms. Northstar, I snatched a glass of Prosecco, almost stepping on a solitary pup before strolling over and sitting down on the yellowed lawn. Yes, the breeder's a nice lady, but I hate doing the yada yada thing. Besides, I was there to watch the kids interview the puppies. See that they chose the right one. Stretching out my legs, my mind drifted to the white noise from the freeway, the view of the overheated valley, the squawking crows gathering on the stone wall. I noticed the pup sitting alone on the patio, watching over his friends like they were his flock. He cleaned himself, shook his fur like a Pantene commercial, and then looked directly into my eyes. His gaze emitted a warmth I don't remember having felt before. My kids started laughing too loud when my legs suddenly turned into an obstacle course. One by one the puppies leapt over, climbed over, some tumbled over, and I even assisted a few. This went on for a few minutes. I turned to look for approval from my kids and there he was staring at me again, like he knew me or I reminded him of someone. I smiled at him and immediately felt stupid catching myself trying to elicit his favor. Not what I was thinking about doing this morning. But then again, destiny doesn't require your consent.

Kate grabbed a puppy from the conga line.

"Dad, this one is so funny! We like him."

The breeder came down and pointed.

"That's Dilly. He's a kook. His twin is right there at your feet."

The other Shibas looked up to see Dilly getting hugged, but they never broke stride, tumbling and laughing, while the newly arrived prospective families began taking mental notes, narrowing their choices, watching the purity of Dally leaping, Sun rolling, Moon chasing, and Blue pouncing.

Time was slipping, and Bear's heart started getting smaller. "What if I don't find my assignment? What if my assignment doesn't see me?" Moon ran over and pushed Bear off the patio with her snout, encouraging him to participate.

"Remember what Mom said? Show freely to the world your true self. Go!"

Lacking the funny bones of Dilly and Dally, or the luminous demeanors of Moon and Sun, Bear got in line and methodically scaled the man's legs. He repeated this a second time, and a third until he again sensed something strange about this man; his scent was not pleasant. English lavender, three female tabbies, two male Siamese, hops, barley, but something else? On his final time around, Bear stopped at the man's ankles. He calmly pawed his way up the man's torso. Animated by his mythical idols, he peered into the man's eyes as his muzzle sniffed long and deep. The man's odor wasn't soothing like Ms. Northstar's Douglas Fir or tingly like the host's eucalyptus; no, the closest scent was the Oregonian stinking iris. Bear started to shiver. His fur stretched upwards. His tail grew taut. He sensed Kit felt the same way when he saw Harriet, the seashell, for the first time.

"Dad? Max and I want Dilly."

The breeder quickly apologized.

"I forgot to mention. Dilly and Dally are twins so I would like to keep them together. If you want to take them both, I mean, if you think you have enough room and energy?"

"Kids, I'm sure we don't have the room for two puppies. See if there's another one you like.

His black raspberry gummy nose scanned my face searching for clues. About my habits, my home, my past? No idea, but he mesmerized me. His eyes spoke like a Van Gogh, contrasting intensity with compassion, questioning without needing an answer, silently disabling my resistance. He looked so content, so present. No words. Even the splendor of his face, each stroke of fur tersely dotted in waves of red sesame, black and cream, from his nose to the arch of each brow embodying purity. The little world of glass I was holding onto felt foolish. Impotent. I lifted him like a boy with his first stuffed animal, touching his softness, feeling his fur against my cold cheeks, smelling that distinctive puppy scent, admiring his angelic air. I searched for a flaw, a weakness in his perfection, and then I froze as he stared back at me and smiled.

When the man put him back down, Bear backed up, jumped off the man's lap and ran back to the stone walkway. "What happened?" He took his post and watched as the logjam of pups burst forth once again with Dilly and Dally leading the way. With Sun and Moon and all the others basking in the attention, the joy and anticipation of this incredible day. The assignments laughing, pointing, drinking. The sky, the sun, the air. Everything was the same but everything changed. Bear saw it in the man's eyes.

My brain raced for an exit, grasping for adages as last-minute bulwarks – when pigs fly, when hell freezes over, when your ass grows a beard? Wait a second! I felt compelled to stand up brush off the seat of my pants wipe away the paw tracks look around for an excuse to leave to say I can't do this because I'm too busy and life is too short and maybe the universe will or maybe it won't or maybe I should have another Prosecco? Kate and Max ran up to me scared we might be leaving without a Dilly OR a Dally! And then without another thought in my head, without any consideration for logic or reason or self-interest, I looked at my kids, and consciously left behind my safe, sane, controlled existence.

I picked him up and walked over to Ms. Northstar. "Who is this?"

"This is Kuma. His real name is Bear, but I call him Kuma. It means "bear" in Japanese. I think he prefers it."

"We'll take him. Kids? Let's go!" *(Looks in Kuma's eyes)* You're going home. *(Hands him to Kate)*

"Dad, can I call him Prince?"

"Kate, can I call you Phoebe? His name is Kuma."

The universe had spoken.

The Blue Leash

"To affect the quality of the day, that is the highest of arts. Every man is tasked to make his life, even in its details, worthy of the contemplation of his most elevated and critical hour."

– Henry David Thoreau

The Walk

Oh, how bright our bungalow glowed with pride for our new fluffy fur boy! I'm surprised the wooden stork didn't soar out from the basement for one more visit on the front lawn. Much like having a toddler, our rooms were baby-proofed and reorganized. Frames and vases placed on higher shelves or relegated downstairs. Baby gates secured in several doorways to prevent flight. And all lower cupboard doors were latched. Then the selfies and videos came out to capture every moving paw as rawhide bones, baby bacon treats, and multi-colored stuffed animals were gifted, his new crate was christened with champagne, and the focus of our lives shifted faster than even we understood at the time.

No more than two nights went by before Kuma suffered a nervous reaction to his anti-virus medication; he began sniffing the floors like a commercial vacuum cleaner. By 1 am, he was whimpering, pacing and jumping ad nauseum. We called the breeder who advised us to watch him, let the medicine take its course, and give him plenty of time and space. So, there we were, Melissa and I, maternity nurses changing shifts every few hours, monitoring our 9-week-old patient through the night. Where's my daughter, you ask?

Let me be fair. The car ride alone, transporting Kuma to his new home, almost made the entire ordeal worth it. From the rearview mirror I watched new versions of Kate and Max, sitting on each side of Kuma's carrier. Kate morphed into a doting mother, opening the front of his carrier to feed him treats, patting his head like a gold star student, and telling him a story of a dog who found the perfect home. My son grew into the concerned father, cautioning Kate not to overfeed Kuma, admonishing Kate for patting him too much and trying to touch his face or paw before she slapped it back. They were engaged, devoted and caring human beings who shared a common bond.

"Kuma, that's a beautiful name. You look like a Kuma. And you're mine."

"Kate, he's ours you said."

"I'm his mother. You're his uncle."

"Kuma, we are going to be best friends."

"Max, leave him alone. He doesn't like you."

"He loves both of us. Don't you Kuma?"

And they talked to him and pet him and sang to him all the way home.

The Blue Leash

Melissa, initially hesitant to expand our family, quickly found her groove with Kuma as well. She had had one dog growing up, Mitzi, whom she felt had filled her dog quota for a lifetime, but she agreed the kids needed a dog. Yet, as soon as Kuma flew out of his carrier, she fell in love with his looks, his curious nature, and his charming aloofness. Along with the kids, she repeatedly burst into laughter while Kuma probed our bedroom, pursued his coiled tail and investigated the feline scent underneath our door. Several times during his orientation, Kuma stopped his search and turned to Melissa, as if he was asking her, "How do you like me now?"

The following morning the kids took on their full responsibility. Waking up earlier than on Christmas morning, Kate crept into our room and cuddled Kuma in his crate, whispering her devotion and petting his oversized, furry head. She even allowed Max a few seconds inside the crate before directing him to get Kuma's kibble breakfast ready while she chaperoned him to the dining room. Then they shadowed him around the house. Sat with him as he stretched. Laughed when he battled my slipper. Fed him treats as he got tired. Laid down with him when he napped. We had to wait one week after his 2nd vaccination before we could walk him so the kids chased Kuma around the backyard, tailing him while he sniffed the honeysuckle and the fenced perimeter. They raced into the house several times reporting every detail about what the "cutest dog ever" just did before running back out to avoid missing his next incredible feat.

The next day we brought Kuma to Grandma Lydia's apartment in Azusa. I finally had convinced my mom to move in 2006, after living in Connecticut by herself for the past thirty years, and our visit to her home that day was one of the happiest moments in her later life. After Kate and Max proudly walked him in, Grandma was completely charmed by every little sniff, leap and pounce. She laughed at "his serious face," pet him *a little too hard*, fed him a few crackers and even though Kuma resisted being held by anyone that afternoon, he allowed her to hold him, instantly putting a twinkle back into my mom's eyes.

Those first few days were ideal. A whirlwind of puppy-inspired happiness. A loving, family honeymoon etched in unending firsts - meeting the cats, playing with a nerf football, observing our neighbors, faux barking, sleeping upside down, hiding under the bed, and spurting, chasing, rolling and boldly ambushing our cats. The kids barely watched TV. Barely whined about "what a boring summer" it was. Little Kuma became the center of their lives and an unexpected elixir for all of us . . . until he wasn't.

What surfaced became an issue led by Kate but voiced by all.

"He's your dog, Dad. All he does is follow you."

"I don't want him to follow me. Did I ask for him to follow me?"

The Blue Leash

"He was supposed to be for me and Kate?"

"Well, that's because I feed him!"

"No, you don't. We do!"

"Then I don't know why he follows me."

"Because you picked him out. You were the first one to touch him. He only loves you."

My wife's eyebrows arched, her arms crossed, her head tilted to the side, tacitly saying everything I didn't want to hear. Hey, no one told me Shiba Inus were extremely loyal, territorial and according to *A Complete Pet Owner's Manual for Shiba Inus*, "will only take one master in his or her lifetime." I didn't think a few treats after the kids went to bed would make him mine forever! Let me offer just one of my early, early journal entries in my defense:

"It's been almost one whole week with Kuma and . . . BIG EFFIN MISTAKE!!! This was one of the worst decisions I've ever made. I am the main caregiver, provider, pooper scooper, feeder and soon-to-be walker, and this dog is an attention grabbing, pig-headed, constant irritation that is disrupting MY LIFE, MY SLEEP, MY RELATIONSHIP WITH MY KIDS AND MY FREE TIME!!"

But they were right. I never confessed our mutual attraction when we picked him out but from day one, Kuma insisted on being my dog. He willed himself to be my dog. In spite of my daughter following through with her promise to be his main caregiver, Kuma clung to me like an extra appendage. Kate's loyalty to Kuma lasted just over a week, but she tried and if I were her, I would have given up as well. Where did my son go? He found time each day to love Kuma and pet him, but Legos were easily more attentive and amenable to his wishes. And so, be it kismet or karma, all Kuma's attention and duties fell to me.

As with all things between love and war, our house began to normalize. Aside from having to adapt to Kuma's stubborn will, his indifference to family and friends, his nipping the ankles of family and friends, and his omnipresence throughout our house and my life, I realized it was better to accept the new world order. Once school started in August, the kids still played with Kuma and occasionally helped with his duties, and my daily to-do list for Kuma required little more than my cat to-do list. The only major difference was having to walk him. Informed by observing the neighbors with their dogs, I thought walking Kuma was nothing more than strolling him around McDonald Park, letting him do his poop, put the poop in a poop bag, and then head back home to resume my life. The walk would also check off the "keeping the dog physically active" box, and Shiba Inus needed only one 30-minute walk per day, so what the hell? Two birds, one walk. Right? Right?

Let the Dance Begin

"Who wants to go for a walk?"

Silence. Five seconds pass.

"Kuma? Kuma?"

The Blue Leash

Shaking his shiny blue leash, I got into the habit of approaching Kuma like Moe from the Three Stooges, narrating aloud, "Slowly I turned, step by step, inch by inch." Kuma would be sprawled on the sofa, pretending to be unaware of my looming ambush, as his ears perked up and rotated like submarine periscopes, while his peripheral vision calculated his swift descent and escape. Kuma hustled me around the dining room, the living room, the coffee table, the hallway and through the kitchen. Three laps. More if he was feeling frisky, less if he was waking from a nap.

"Come on, Dad. Catch me!"

"Kuma! I don't have time for this."

"You can't catch me!"

"Do you want to go for a walk or what?"

He sped up from slow to hurried. Hurried to fast. Fast to manic. Have you ever seen a manic Shiba Inu? Feint to the left. Juke to the right. Leap. Feint and juke, flip. Feint, leap, juke, flip and feint. As soon as I gave up and told him we're not going, he would slink over to the front door and sit, waiting for me to put on his leash.

"So, why did we do all that? We wasted five precious minutes! What was the point?"

My frustration reminded me of Emerson's belief how "every man's [dog's] condition is a solution in hieroglyphic to those inquiries he would put." Well, my inquiries into Kuma's decipherable, elliptical chases were plentiful: why does his body shimmy during this dance? What's with the impish eye contact? The little grin as he circles the proverbial bases? What about the high-speed, windshield wiper motion of his tail? I know these are all signs but as Emerson explained, they needed to be decoded and for the first few years, well, I didn't care. Some days all this was cute and endearing but most days, not so much; I just thought it was a waste of time. It took me years to understand it was anything but a waste of time.

Once we stepped off the porch, I'd scan my watch to determine how much time I had to give up for this walk. Left towards the park? Quick. Right towards all the doggie neighbors? 30 minutes. North to the ambitious, uphill route? 40 minutes. Or east to the longer, straight route? 50 minutes. Will Kuma be more Santa Anita racehorse to get back for dinner or Gary the Snail because he doesn't understand time? It eventually didn't matter, though, because it was Kuma's walk, so I always felt it should be his choice.

From the time he came home, I resisted being Kuma's master, or his pack leader, as if he needed someone to rule over him. Yes, his six-week training seemed essential, like teaching a kindergartener to sit, to take turns talking, and to raise their hand whenever they needed to go to the bathroom. The basics. But Kuma's trainer was straight *Full Metal Jacket*, as if anything less than total mind control would be unacceptable. Either obey her commands 150% or Kuma would make me his bitch.

The Blue Leash

"The leash must never be tight! When you are walking, never stop. Show him you are in charge. At home you eat first. Ignore your dog when you walk into a room. He must know YOU are the alpha dog! UNDERSTAND?" No, I didn't.

I never bought into the Tarzan-like mantra of "Me-teacher! You-student!" My approach to Kuma mirrored my teaching philosophy with high school juniors. It is a give-and-take relationship. I will respect you and listen to you, but I ask you to do the same for me. If you have three tests today, I'll move our quiz to tomorrow, but we work harder the next class. You can't concentrate because your best friend betrayed you during lunch? I'll give you the notes after class, but you still need to do tonight's homework. Maybe you woke up in a good mood and want to walk two miles instead of one? Fine, but give me time to do schoolwork tonight. And so, I tried to make our walks a collaboration of my teaching sense and Kuma's gift for scents but a few obstacles still got in the way.

Kuma's nose chose a different route every day, but once he decided, he put on his game face, got "into the zone" and proceeded to stand still. If I was writing his college recommendation, the first words to describe him would be "naturally curious, stubbornly determined and easily distracted by nature." Considering we were "walking," it drove me CRAZY how Kuma spent the first 5 minutes STANDING in front of our house! Sniffing rocks, licking leaves, logging information. Sometimes, if we only had

30 minutes, a hard tug on the leash was needed to move him along, and he would begrudgingly carry on, but there were many times when a dog's urine or coyote's poop ranked top priority, needing an immediate and thorough investigation. It didn't matter what I said or did; Kuma would not budge.

Kuma's unpredictable pace also became a serious bone of contention between us on our walks. Some days he slowed down to show me he was the alpha male or possibly to be obstinate for his own pleasure. I would plead; he would ignore. There were times when I had a full night of grading papers. Kuma chose those times to linger and roll on a neighbor's newly mulched lawn. I would bark; he would stare. Other times school days overflowed with parent meetings, faculty in-services or an entire day of disorderly classes. I'd go home ready for a meandering walk to relax but magically, those were the days Kuma chose to rush around the park for barely a few sniffs before returning home. When it came to my time, he was definitely not giving; he was only taking.

Great. So, every day we're taking his walk on his route, stopping when he wants, and going at his pace. What about me? What was I supposed to do during these olfactory tours? Aside from picking up his clumps of clay sculptures, how might I profit or be productive while giving up my personal time? I can't grade papers. Can't create lesson plans, power points or answer parent emails. Can't prep dinner.

The Blue Leash

Got it! Again, by neighborly observation, I learned to put in my earbuds and zone out. I'd plug into politics, sports or Spotify. While Kuma lurched like a metro bus, stopping at every bush, rock and furry butt, I moved without thinking or feeling, quite pleased for taking control of my time.

In that first year and slightly beyond, I resented Kuma for taking away my free time. How he suddenly became my responsibility. How my life became subservient to his whims, dictated by his necessities, hijacked by his desires, for 30-60 minutes every single day. Maybe other people like this, but not me. Other people who have no lives, family or friends, but not me. I didn't mind feeding him or taking him to the vet. Maybe throw him the ball after dinner for a few minutes in the backyard but walking him every day, sometimes twice a day? No, no, no. That was my time!

My time.

I don't know exactly when "my time" became a thing. Reading Seneca's "Shortness of Life" years ago might have influenced me, though, as he explained man's disquiet regarding the brevity of life is not "that we have a short space of time, but that we waste much of it," and believe me, I hate wasting time. Maybe after twenty years of being a teacher, after donating countless hours to the altruistic cause, I resented anyone else infringing on my personal life. Being that I'm getting quite old, it could be time's value naturally increases exponentially. Maybe the time spent on computers and social media has conditioned me, where anything taking more than a nanosecond raises my anxiety and frustration? Or maybe I've always been selfish with my time.

It was mid-October, first quarter grades were due, when the flu knocked me out for a week. Whenever I get sick, I get curmudgeon-like – impatient, constantly swearing, angry over the smallest things – and instantly repel anyone who loves me out of my sight. Nevertheless, Kuma weathered my verbal storms and anchored himself on the bed the entire time. Periodically, he checked my eyes, sniffed my mouth, and laid back down like a selfless, live-in caregiver, and despite my family's best efforts and my insistent yelling for him to go, he refused to walk with anyone else. He only wanted to walk with me, which made me angrier, of course, because I couldn't understand why he would sacrifice his own pleasure for my sake.

After a few days, wrapped in layers of clothes and self-pity, I rose above my infirmity to lead Kuma around the park for a walk. Firmly harnessing him, often pulling on his leash, I hustled around our thirty-minute route hoping to do it in twenty. Somewhere between the "Keep Your Pet Off Our Lawn" house and the year-round Christmas lights house, Kuma decided to meet Gloria, an older Latina woman, who was sweeping her front sidewalk. Rather than passing her by, on his way to his wild rosemary bush, Kuma uncharacteristically stopped to sniff her weathered legs. Comforted by Kuma's interest, she smiled. "Muy bonita." "Yes, he is," I said, "but – " and tears began walking down her cheeks. She had buried

The Blue Leash

her third dog last week. "Can't have anymore. Like children. Hurts too much." I reached back to high school. "Lo siento." She grinned, knowing no other words, and sweetly hugged us both, and kissed Kuma's forehead before shuffling her feet back up her fractured driveway. Kuma stared at me like I stare at my class after my most passionate, meaningful lecture. I returned to school the following day.

A few weeks later, on an early morning walk, we didn't go five hundred steps before Kuma doggedly refused to take another step. He had begged me to go for a walk and now he balked like a Gen Z child. Like he wanted to receive unmerited adulation or renegotiate the terms of his social contract before moving another paw. "DO YOU WANT TO JUST GO BACK HOME?" Failing to coax him with an ALL CAPS yell, hurtful words shot out of my mouth ending with something like, "I have a life, too, you know!" When he finally got up to walk again, his front right paw flinched. And flinched. And flinched again. The tiny burr in his paw pad should have launched pain-expelling yelps, but he was silent. After pulling out the thorns, Kuma's only response was to glow at me with adoration, like I was his hero. Slipping through shades of guilt, shame and remorse, I knelt down and attempted to stare into his soul. "I'm sorry. I wasn't paying attention." He looked at me and quietly absolved me of all my sins with grace and a smile.

These moments of canine humanity awakened me to recognize my selfish nature, a blameless poser who often sees himself as a put-upon innocent. The defensive chip on my shoulder, the self-righteous impatience, the license I give myself to judge everyone for lacking self-reliance, for not picking themselves up by the bootstraps. "Oh, what a tangled web we weave," especially when we deceive ourselves and yet, for some reason, these moments with Kuma sparked me to edify myself and change my life. How effortless he made forgiveness. How simple it was to choose empathy and understanding. How happy I became walking with Kuma.

I soon noticed during school, while my students were writing an in-class essay or taking a test, I would catch myself looking at the wall clock, thinking about going home to walk Kuma. Anticipating his greeting when I walked in the house. Waiting for the dance to begin again. Once a bane in my life, like an ex-smoker preaching the truth, the walk became my refuge. It became our ritual. Each afternoon I left my earbuds behind to watch him enjoy the natural world in a way I rarely enjoyed anything in my life. His rhythmic gait marched on like a disciple experiencing his first pilgrimage. His eyes gathered approaching stimuli with a mix of curiosity and street smarts. His delicate nose questioned each petal, each leaf, and every storied palm frond. Everything he sniffed, everything he passed, everyone he saw, he absorbed with delight, with an existential satisfaction, and he emitted it back out to the world twofold.

"Dad, slow down. This one is important!"

"No problem, Kuma. Take your time."

The Blue Leash

Seeing the walk through Kuma's eyes allowed me to shed my guarded persona and limiting desires and helped me recognize how essential these mini-excursions were for his well-being. Not only to just get out of the house or relieve himself. Not to keep his hips active (Shibas have hereditary hip issues), but every walk reaffirmed his identity and license to the outside world. When he was sniffing a plant or a lamppost, he was reading a text from his neighborhood pals. No different than scrolling down my Facebook wall or checking my friends' Instagram stories. He would leave a comment, maybe a thumbs up, and move to the next post. When he stopped to observe other dogs, he looked to get their attention, or maybe to say hi as they passed on opposite sides of the street. "Sniff you next time!" And every once in a while, he would turn and look at me. Without judgement, without expectations. Two old guys enjoying each other's company, like we were going out for a beer together after work. But this newfound friendship, this communion of souls, did not come naturally. It was only when I let go of my needs and *let myself* see the walk through his eyes. That's when the magic of our relationship began.

Until Kuma's joy became my joy, the universe was only as big as my tiny, self-defensive lens saw it. I was living on cruise control, emphasis on control. I was a father and a husband, ready to do whatever a father and husband does, but my life changed when I saw the value in Kuma's life. When I understood Kuma was more than a dog or a pet. Once

I shifted my perspective, and resuscitated my connection to the natural world, it wasn't his Mexican feather grass; it was ours. It wasn't his park; it was a place we could enjoy together.

Almost two years slipped by before Kuma's walks unlocked a joy long forgotten in my trip to adulthood. Where "few adult persons can see nature," Kuma invited me to be a boy once again. A boy who climbed trees, who rode bikes, who ran for the sheer joy of running. Who lived for the outdoors rather than in a car or behind a desk. To breathe the complexities of the air and rely on my senses to translate the world. I wasn't trying to fit the walk into my life anymore; I started fitting my life around the walk. I had learned, as Eva Hoffman mentions in her famous treatise on time, how even "as we try to get the maximum use of every minute, we end up getting no use out of them at all." Even Kuma's chase before each walk became decipherable; it was to engage me, to get me excited before the walk so I would walk WITH him. Inviting me to let go of all the daily confrontations and senseless aggressions. Letting go of phones, computers, emails and the unnatural ideal of multi-tasking. To wander the neighborhoods without caring where we went or how long it might take. To throw a ball, to chase a bug, to meet a stranger, to sit on a bench, to linger on Chester, to prance on Washington, to forage the outskirts of McDonald Park, to yodel at a raccoon, to slow down when it rains. To share the earth, the divinity of Nature, with Kuma, distant from every person, everything extraneous and mundane. To finally let go of my time.

The Blue Leash

The Dream

The dream engulfed us all.

He bore an absolute presence,
In motion and in rest,
Radiant, wise, omniscient.

He wore exquisite, vivid colors
Of red sesame, black, and cream
Repainting the faded promises of life.

There was an ethereal breath,
Of Genesis proportions,
Short, measured, comforting.

There was a sparkling joi of vivre,
Born and graced Muditâ,
Unbridled, inclusive, spontaneous.

There was a true selfless love,
From a sinless divinity,
Eyes feeding our spirits with manna.

And then one night.
A nightmare engulfed all of us.
Stillness.
Still.

> "*Death is not the greatest loss in the world.
> The greatest loss is what dies inside us while we live.*"
> **– Norman Cousins**

The Blue Leash

Journal #1
December 15, 2019
thru January 19, 2020

. . . like a boy who lost his best friend . . . like a dad who lost a son . . . a spouse who lost their soulmate . . . a sexagenarian who momentarily lost his will to live.

December 15 (12:30 a.m.)

Kuma Bear, our supernatural fur boy, born on May 23rd, 2008, has died tonight, on December 14th, 2019 at 11:44 p.m. at the Foothill Emergency Hospital. The absolute <u>LOVE</u> of my life! The <u>One</u>! Kuma Bear has died, and I am alone once again in the human world. This gorgeous hunk of Shiba Inu, who graced our lives for 11 ½ years, has left the earth.

Scott D. DoVale

My best friend, traveling companion, circus clown, personal therapist, camp director and zen master. You healed me with your aloe vera fur, a knowing glance, a Spidey sense of empathy, always curling next to me at the perfect time. I never realized you were the axis of my daily life. Waking to feed you, walk you, hug you, chase you, and talk with you every day and night. This void will stretch past tomorrows, next weeks and years until my own demise. I don't know where you are, but I pray you know how much I cherished you. Even though I was blessed to hug you & kiss you for a solid week before you left, a few pieces of me died with you – a lighter heart, a truer laugh, a kinder spirit.

It will take years for me to put into words how your loyalty and love transformed my life, but they will just be words. What I feel right now (strange that it comes so late) is I needed you as much, if not more, than you needed me. Just like Steinbeck's George & Lennie, in *Of Mice and Men*, weaving together friendship and dependence. In the family, there was Melissa (my wife, your Mom), two incredible children, Kate and Max, and there was you. And then there was me. I'll carry you with me at least until I get Alzheimer's. Why should I even retire if you're not home with me? That was the plan, remember? Can't thank you enough for being the yin to my yang. For giving me everything I never knew I needed when I needed it. For being you. I love you, Kuma!

The Blue Leash

December 15 (7:52 am)

WHAT JUST HAPPENED? Sunday morning. First morning without you. Ten hours have passed. The house is so disturbingly quiet. Not that you ever made noise. You never barked, growled, shouted, tore pillows, shattered vases, played music too loud. Too chill for all that. Maybe extensive toenail tapping on the hardwood floors once in a while but . . . o.k., you definitely went ballistic when the mailman shoved the letters through the mail slot. You ripped the shit out of our mail, BUT you were ultimate ninja! Your absence magnifies the innate silence of our house right now. And what's the new dawn without you? Less to do, less to worry about, less to love. Reminds me of the day we dropped off Kate at UC Santa Cruz, when existential loss crashed into my chest like Thor's hammer. Anxiety attack #1. Or when Mom and I kissed Max goodbye on his new campus in NOLA, before boarding the St. Charles streetcar back to the hotel. Anxiety attack#2. "Love ten, hurt ten." I'm keeping your bowls in the kitchen, your crate in the bedroom, and your spirit in my heart. The hard part now is telling the kids. After your diagnosis, they believed (as I did) that we would be together for our family New Year's and many months beyond. It will be a total shock. As it is right now.

This pitiful morning lacks your wiggly butt, your breakfast 360s, your laser stare directing me to open the back door for your first pee, and your profusion of plush fur to nuzzle my nose. I will miss your daily routine of leaping down from our bed to the sofa, the yard, and your bed. Then a long walk, back to the sofa, your dinner, my dinner, the fireplace rug, back to the sofa and finally back to bed. I will miss your perfect ears. I will miss your soul loving me unconditionally. I will miss your delicious, toothy smile with your left fang hanging out. Did you hang that fang out on purpose? Like a woman who drapes her hair over one eye? Seductive Shiba! You had me at woof! I will miss your greeting at the front door, flopping into your upside-down, flying Superman pose. Watching you on the Kuma-cam when I'm at school. Feeling your weighty presence sleeping between the two of us every night. And I'm still . . .

What just happened . . . what the f--- just happened?

December 15 (3:18 pm)

Conversations etching time. I called Kate in Santa Cruz. Kate, as you know, is quite tough on the outside, but a marshmallow on the inside. (Remember when she trembled and cried when she saw her first dead squirrel on the road?) On the phone, her voice quivered as I'm sure her body did the same. Shock begot silence before "When did he die? . . . How did you know to take him? . . . Are you o.k., Dad? . . . How's Mom taking it? . . . I can't believe he's gone." The silences, never heard between us before, were filled with your absence, this dearth of comprehension deepening our love for you and each other.

The Blue Leash

I texted Max, "Are you home?" He texted back, "Something wrong?" He's been in New Orleans since August. It's his first semester at Loyola. He came home for Thanksgiving so he knew you were sick. And he's coming home in less than two days for Christmas. On the phone, his responses between the tears, sniffles and pauses. "What? . . . I thought this might happen . . . I prayed I would get to see him when I got home . . . Are you o.k.? . . . How's mom? . . . Can I call you back?" And then I'm sure he cried a multitude of tears in a private hour of his own.

December 15 (10:50 pm)
Walked your favorite route (#1) this morning – up Chester, over to Bell, up Michigan, west across Washington, down Mar Vista and then – HEY, there's Michael, the physics teacher from school I rarely talk to, and HEY, there's me with your aged blue leash wrapped around my hand hugging him and shedding tears on his chest. Awkward, but so be it. I swear I'm not letting you go. I'm keeping your Shiba vibe in my heart. Damn it!! Whose fur face will I kiss in the dark, dark, darkness when I go to bed? I still can't fathom losing you. The distance between us is sooooo effing palatable right now. I'm trying to catch you before you leave, to bring you back, to hold onto you and remember everything, but it feels like I'm somehow falling behind.

The office rug lays breathless. The dining room poses as an abandoned community theater set. Even solitude's warmth feels estranged. The vacant house, the inanimate blandness, the smell of abysmal loss. Everything about us is dissipating, like the remnants of a fantastic dream after the alarm jars you awake, like the memories are all fading and seeping, and I can't stop them. The lifeblood of our home is drip, drip, dripping away (here comes Van Morrison's *Hymns to the Silence*). Oh, beautiful boy, let me reel in your leash and hold your body tight. I pray your soul is alive and finds peace. Please wait for me! I'll be looking for you first when I die (sorry Mom and Dad!). Also, I will be walking our walk every day for one year. I thought of this when we came back from the hospital last night. 11 ½ years = 1 year of walks. I will never forget. Good night, Prince!

December 16 (3 a.m.)

While lying in bed, staring at the ceiling in the dark, flipping through albums of memories in my head, I posed a simple question to myself, "Favorite memory?" Rifling through moments of your life - puppy, teen, life coach, senior citizen – until one of them halted the search. Every night after Melissa went to bed, as our fortress drifted to sleep, as silence turned golden, I would be in the office – reading, grading, prepping for tomorrow's class – and nine nights out of ten, when I looked out of these office doors, you'd be sitting in the dining room's darkness, staring at me like a guardian angel, as if you were divinely assigned to watch over me. For protection and guidance. That's what I wanted to believe.

The Blue Leash

You came to change my life. 39 ½ lbs. of devotion. Priceless. Or maybe you were hoping to ask me a.) if I wanted to play with the Nerf football or b.) if I wanted to go outside or c.) if I would feed you a little more, maybe a snack and . . . and . . . I'm sorry. My brain just unplugged. I fear Banquo's ghost. Back to bed.

December 16 (11:45 pm)

I'm anticipating another sleepless night. Not feeling your weight at the end of the bed feels eerie, like our queen bed expanded into a large king. Thinking about "Princess and the Pea," and my pea is gone. The past few nights have given me a glimpse into the nocturnal world of our neighborhood raccoons, coyotes and owls. I whisper your name like the Santa Anas but there is no response. "Where is a voice to answer mine back? Where are two [paws] that click to my clack? I'm all alone in the world!" (Thank you, Mr. Magoo).

Your Mom and I marked your transition at Lucky Baldwin's tonight, drinking a few Belgian beers, still in shock as we replay the night before and how blessed we were to share in your divinity. Then we came home and cried in each other's arms like we've never cried before. Like we've never cried before. Since exchanging our vows in 1993, we've never shared pain so personally devastating to both of us. You are the most significant family member, from OUR family, that we've lost. And it was so sudden. And then we . . . and then we . . . say wha? We did wha? We created your shrine! Using grandma Betty's side table, we placed the two tall, glass vases of fur you had shed (and I had gathered) in the center, which I originally displayed in my classroom, and we added red votive candles, your squeaky Christmas bone, your blue leash, a few pine cones, and the picture of you playing Trivial Pursuit with us on Christmas, 2016. We had a few more Belgians by your bed, relived indelible flashes of your puppy days, how perfectly you fit into the family, how much we loved you, how much you loved me, how empty our lives feel right now. Heartbroken. Disbelieving. Did not see this coming.

*It's not that I didn't have enough time with you;
I just wanted more time with you.*

December 18

The magic has left the building. One glance, one smile, one tail sweep, and as effective as the M.I.B.'s Neurolyzer, the day's problems were erased in Kumaville, the land of tug toys, chew bones and belly scratches. I might have experienced a day of non-responsive classes, cheating students, long ass faculty meetings, and cursed my way home through the worst drivers ever, but when I opened the front door -- Ba-BAM! Upside down wiggle! Circle the sofa! Jump on my leg! Always excited, happy, unbridled animation. Every single day you brought joy into my life. *Heaven*.

Also, after a few days of retrospect, I'm grateful for how you extended my life as a dad. Ever since I was a teen, my only aspirations revolved around being a dad, and after the years of raising Max and Kate were over, you still needed me. Days when you were throwing up grass, nights when the thunder shook the house, or when your medication had adverse effects. Times you needed someone to toss the frisbee with or play tug-of-war. Oh, Kuma Bear. I will miss this life-affirming chapter in my life. Raising Kuma! Can't fathom never seeing you again. Wish I could kiss you again and again. Forehead. Eyes. Nose. Good night, Prince.

December 24

Ten days. Your life is vanishing as the hours rush to the holiday, while my life unwillingly acclimates itself to having "one less enchanted object." Our relationship fading as time insists on erasing the significance of our shared lives. This is what I'm fighting against today, tomorrow, every day, every walk – to secure your memory. To make your life resonate in my soul long after your death. It's easy right now to recall you sniffing sage brush along the sidewalks, or pursuing the snowy white poodle on Mar Vista, or your persistent peeing on the stone lamppost in the park, but what about next month? In six months? Will I be able to conjure up your impish smile on a whim? Will I always have that power, or will it go the way of everything else? I hate this shit, this life without. When you meet the buddha on the road . . . I know. I've lived for 64 years, but my only wish right now is that you knew in the last minute of your life, and even now, how much I love you. How beyond dog you were for me. Listening to Jimmy Eat World's "Hear You Me" – "You gave [me] someplace to go / I never said thank you for that . . . May angels lead you in." That's the crux of my pain. Don't think I said thank you enough. Or I love you enough . . . afraid I let you down . . . we always think we have more time . . . or more walks . . . so afraid I let you down.

December 25 (noon)

Christmas. Coffee. Presents. Mom's green chili frittata. Cook all day. Watch NBA games. Prime rib dinner with popovers. *Mr. Magoo's Christmas Carol*. The gravity of your absence lies in all of them. The family's whispered silences this morning were palpable as every tear of wrapping paper underscored the desolation. Every shout of surprise singed with sadness. Which is not to say we withdrew into an all-day vigil of novenas and chest beatings, but as I've learned many times over, the indifferent world stops for no one. Missed you sitting with the kids when they opened presents. Most of the time you sat patiently between them, filling in the gaps when they sat there wondering, "How long do we gush about this present before we can open another one?" And you always made us laugh when you opened your presents – bones and stuffed animals delighted you every time.

After gifts and breakfast, I walked outside and stared at the house across the street. The one I rented for the

The Blue Leash

last two years of Grandma's life while she battled liver cancer. You were almost three years old when I started bringing you over as my surrogate. Especially in those last six months, I managed her basic needs while you handled her emotional support. Max visited every day to keep her company and play the piano. Mom and Kate brought conversation and See's chocolate. And you laid on her medical bed, like her personal nurse or guardian, letting her stroke your medicinal fur again and again. Thank you, Kuma. Merry Christmas, Mom.

I turned the corner towards our ceremonial walk around McDonald Park. Weather was perfectly you. Crisp, blue sky. Not too sunny, not quite sweater. It's always great weather on Christmas, but I would never know if we didn't take our walk. It was my one chance to be outside before cooking all day in the kitchen. Today I laughed about last Christmas when you stopped and sat your ass down on the sidewalk because I refused to go the way you wanted. I immediately sat my ass down right next to you, mocking your face and posture. We looked like two, old stubborn men waiting for the other one to yodel "Uncle!"

When I walked by the empty basketball court, I finally conceded there wasn't a perfect time for you to die. Maybe for you, but I was in too deep. It wasn't the hour or the day of the week; it was the loss. At the adjoining lamppost, tears inched, then avalanched down my cheeks recalling your intense fascination with this one post. It was there you taught me to slow my motor down, to pay more attention to details, and I learned the "give and take" in a relationship. Now you're teaching me what devastating loss feels like, and how clinging to pain can satisfy one's soul. Everybody hurts, right? Thank you, Sensei.

December 26 (1 am)

Woke up with the same thoughts I've had every night since you left – I miss how you intentionally stepped on my legs in the morning before jumping down from the bed, so I would wake up and serve you breakfast. I miss you visiting me on the toilet if I took too long like you were worried something happened to me. I miss you laying on the porch, begging for treats in the den, rolling on the lawn, chasing flies in the house, sleeping with the cats. None of the cable channels, including HBO, entertained me like you.

Struggling with your absence #103 – Tonight I'm wrapped up in your Lakers beach towel, the one a few of my students gave you for Christmas. They presented it to me after school on Thursday, the 12th, the last day of exams. They didn't understand why I started crying until I told them, "Kuma's very sick. I don't know how much longer he has, but . . . thank you so much for the towel and his stocking of toys." We all cried for you, not knowing you were going to die two days later.

Struggling with your absence #104 – Trying to stop talking about you to Max and Kate. They insist it's fine, and

The Blue Leash

they've been very understanding about my apparent gloom. Actually, we've all been sharing our heartbreak with our favorite Kuma stories. I can see Melissa and the kids are struggling with their pain as well, while consoling me for mine. Once we go back to our post-holiday lives, I'm sure we will all have our own tears to shed. I also know your absence will cut even deeper when the kids go back to their schools, and the nest becomes emptier than it's ever been. Shit. Shit. Shit.

Tonight's 10-Minute Kuma Poetry Entry – *Shedding*

Before you go
Let me kiss your nose
To tell you I will miss you.
Before you go
Let me look into your eyes
To tell you I will always love you.
Before you go
Let me cast my head onto yours
To tell you I don't want you to leave.
Before you go
Let me lift you in my arms
To share your pain
To share my pain
To hold you back –
Until I can go with you.

December 26

"That was YOU, wasn't it? *"It was a Christmas miracle!"* You weren't the annoying fly divebombing my face at my desk last night, were you? No, and you weren't the clawing sound in the wall next to the fireplace. No, that's the raccoon family. You remember right before Grandma died, she threatened, I mean *promised*, to come back as a butterfly? Well, it's been years, and I still can't tell if she's one of the butterflies in our backyard. Never gave it much credence but now?

These past twelve days I've been asking for a sign – a touch, a vision, a text – to tell me you're ok, and as you may know, last night brought me to my knees. In case it wasn't you . . . sleep left me around 2:30 this morning. It usually puts its clothes on and exits like an old lover but this was different. I tossed and turned. Rock and rolled. Punched my pillow into balloon animals. Finally got up around 3:30, rechecked the door locks, the battened down hatches, the blown-out candles. The glow from the office?

"Weird? I shut the computer around midnight."

I popped my head into the dark, and bright as a full moon, what did I see? Your luminous Shiba face glowing back at me on my desktop! Your twinkling, cloudy eyes smiling upside down on the living room floor, four days before you died. *My favorite picture of all time.* Staring at me in the silence, I started projecting supernatural implications on your pixels, before accepting what was and what isn't anymore.

"It's you and me again. But I'm tired, and you're not here."

I shut off the computer and headed to bed, grateful for what was until over my shoulder I see the glow parting the office doors. *Black Mirror*? *Punk'd*? Was I chasing you once again?

"What the hell?"

More awake than not, I confirmed the computer was back on. *Twilight Zone*? I shut your face off again, waited at least 15 seconds before I slowly turned to go and . . . *he's back*!!! I sighed heavily, inhaling hope, expelling doubt. To believe in something greater, to feel a mystical moment, beyond sanity or reason, but maybe I shut it down too fast? I laughed at the absurdity, absorbing your image one more time as I said good night. I held down the off button emphatically, tinged with irritability, but as soon as I turned . . . instantly, and I mean INSTANTLY, you returned. That endearing smile shattered my skepticism as I fell to my knees. "It's you, isn't it?" *(Tears. A grateful smile.)* Don't worry, Bear. I'll never let you go." The impromptu vigil began, thanking God and the universe, the angels and saints, savoring your celestial presence. Until the off button was pressed one last time.

December 28

THE TRUTH IS MY DOG DIED. THE TRUTH IS I FEEL SOMEWHAT LOST AND DISCONNECTED FROM LIFE WITHOUT HIM.

I'm seriously mourning the loss of my dog. Not when my uncle hanged himself. Not when my best friend, Rosie, was shot and murdered in Belize. Not when my mother or father died. No one's passing has felt this deep, this disorienting. Kuma's death blindsided me, and I don't know why. Did I not get to say what I wanted to? I did. Did I not tell him I loved him a dozen times a day? I ALWAYS told him. What would I do if I was mourning the passing of Kate? Buy a new Prius, start composting and stop using water? If it was Max, would I play Xbox for hours, listen to Bill Evans and Chet Baker, and compose music for the rest of my life? How can you possibly honor one's death who gave you so much? Or do you just "live your life!" That's what they would want you to do! Ahhhhhh! I HATE that response!!!

(9 pm) Two days after your sudden transition, I went to *Shogun Tattoo* and asked Andrew to embellish the tattoo of your face he did back in July. Yes, me, the same guy who proudly swore to his daughter three years ago, "I'll never get a tattoo. What's the point?" Two weeks to the day, my left deltoid now has "*Kuma*" scripted underneath your face, surrounded by billowy, blue clouds, two red hearts, and a golden halo. Only wish I had a bigger deltoid, but it's beautiful. When he finished tears streamed from the tattoo parlor out into the street. Meant even more when Andrew teared up as well. He mentioned his "dearest girl," Elke, his mini-Aussie shepherd, who passed last October, the day

The Blue Leash

before his 50th birthday. His voice got smaller, talking like he lost his soul. He pulled out several photo albums of Elke he keeps on his workbench. We confessed that we cried more for you and Elke than when our mothers died. Not proud of it. Confused by it, actually, but several other friends have told me they had the same response. At least now you WILL be with me forever.

December 30

Rolled up to the Hyatt Santa Barbara around 3 to begin our traditional New Year's retreat. This was the first hotel you ever stayed in with us. Also, the first road trip you ever took. The kids kept groaning in the car every time you repositioned yourself in the backseat - laying your head on their laps, or standing on them like a captain on his ship, looking out the front windshield. Curious, stoic, trusting your dad as the world whisked by at 80 mph.

What's crazy is the universe took over today. We were given the Santa Rosa room, the same room as on that first trip. Unbelievable. Kate laughed as we walked in, reminding us how you surprised everyone by jumping up on the bed, which you had never done before. It was like watching a child take their first step. Then, after claiming your position next to the window, you turned your head and looked at us, "This bed's mine! Is that a problem?" Never.

For most people, New Year's means going to a party, drinking champagne and making resolutions doomed to never see the first of February. For our family, though, it was a time to be together, away from all our daily distractions. To eat, laugh, talk, and share time together. For me, it was a chance to be a husband and a father. To be a sherpa for all, but especially for you. To carry your water bowl. To walk you 2-3 times a day. Pee and poop you. Bring you to the beach while the family went here and there. It all goes by so fast.

"Life is what happens to you while you're busy making other plans." Right. And death is part of life. Also, true. But as I sit here on East Beach, as the ocean breeze slaps my face, as the setting sun streaks orange, as my pen and journal beg for my thoughts and feelings, you are conspicuously absent. I accept life will be less, much less, from now on, without you, but how long will this implanted pain persist? Will this lingering, bewildering weight become an invisible appendage? I don't mind but I've never felt like this before. And why you? I mean I love you tremendously, but . . .

December 31

*"Two things in life change you, and you are never the same:
Love and Grief."*

A Day of Ashes. Where's my Kuma? Are you in heaven? Are you getting enough to eat? Do you still need your Apoquel? We ate lunch at Shoreline Cafe. Toasted your absence with a Bloody Jerry's, but I missed gazing at you lying next to us on the sand. We followed up lunch with our annual pilgrimage to Pirate's Cove; the first time you weren't by my side. It was high tide so we walked up the cliffs and took the wooden stairs down to the beach. As we got to our treasured secluded spot with your ashes, we didn't need to consciously set a tone; it followed us there. We stood in a circle. Kate started us off by reading a poem. Max was feeling a bit overwhelmed to share his thoughts so I read his beautiful Instagram tribute to Kuma, and then we all contributed anecdotal Cliff Notes of your radiant life before releasing about 10% of your ashes into the breeze, as I was unwilling to let go of you once again, wanting your ashes to stay with us at home. I'm glad I can miss you, and feel how life, and my life, is less without you, because I can tell one day life will feel normal without you. That's when I will lose hope in life.

Dear Lord, I thank you for our beautiful family. Please take care of my boy, Kuma, who was a You send. As Elizabeth Proctor says to her husband in The Crucible, (favorite movie scene of all time), "I never knew such goodness in the world!" I pray, I pray, I pray I never forget this boundless love, this bond of companionship. I have no idea what this new year will bring - whatever joy or darkness it may carry – but I hope to feel the pain of his death every day. To wake in gratitude, to grow in empathy, to remind me how every person I meet quietly carries their pain as well. Believe me, my imagination stands befuddled at my obvious distress, but I remain steadfast in accepting my visceral reaction. To never let go of what was true.

Scott D. DoVale

January 1st, 2020

Living and Breathing

He walked me.
He walked ME.
He showed me things I never saw.
He showed me lamp posts I had totally ignored.
He showed me bushes, trees, parks, and
landscapes that never existed.
He showed me lizards, spiders, rocks, leaves and fallen
palm fronds (that he would piddle on).
One time he showed me the fattest turkey I'd ever seen.
And the biggest raccoon.
Up close and personal.
Another time he forced me to look at
a squirrel's dead body. And a dead crow.

I met people in my neighborhood because of him.
I met an elegant, Kate Hepburn-ish, 78-year-old Sally,
with her two little black schipperkes, Antony and Cleo,
who led her in syncopated patter, beholden only to their
whims, miniature dreams, and Sally's cane.
We talk once a week.

I met a 70-something Asian widow, who briskly walks
her property to water her garden children, including
the 5 large Festucas along the sidewalk. Her 14-year-old

The Blue Leash

Pomeranian, Kareshi, yaps through her screen door. She secretly feeds Kuma treats from her housecoat pocket and laughs. We talk twice a week.

I met a young, professional, 30-ish interracial couple, Kayla and Eric, usually on Sunday mornings. Beaming with parental joy, walking their prized, cream-colored Shiba puppy, who lit up whenever he saw Kuma. Kuma lit up whenever he saw them. Positive, kind energy.

I met a round, graying dude with a gray parka and a round, gray bulldog. He always grunted hello, smiled at Kuma. We never really talked, but we saw each other all the time.

I met Max, a 14-year-old English Mastiff. A huge, white mammal (?) with a "dead man walking" cadence, the kindest soul, beloved by his owner, and taking his life one step at a time. Arthritis diminished his mobility but not his grace and stature. I wish we saw him more.

I met a few resilient homeless men and women, squatting in the shadows of our park, always taking a few steps to greet us, always grateful to share in the joys of a dog's sublime company.

I met young neighbors, old neighbors, new parents supervising the swings, taco cart vendors, AYSO players

and parents, mail persons, walkers, runners, bikers, city
workers, domestic workers, and strangers of every breed.

> See, I am not built to initiate walks or runs
> outdoors or meet new people.
> I am built to read about these connections.
> I am built to read Emerson and Thoreau, who believed
> our souls to be one with the trees and everything Nature.
> I am built to thrive in an insulated environment.
> I am built to sit on the beach and read a book
> or listen to music.

> See, I am not built to initiate walks or runs
> outdoors or meet new people.
> It was Kuma that brought me outside and
> helped me appreciate life again.
> It was Kuma who woke me,
> who made me see more, smell more.
> It was Kuma who made me listen to the
> rhythmic break in a subtle wash to the shore
> and smell the intoxicating ocean scent.
> It was Kuma who patiently helped me live once again.

> See, I am not built to initiate walks or runs
> outdoors or meet new people.
> I am built to sit in hotel rooms, watch sports,
> and eat at the closest café.

The Blue Leash

I am built to visit book stores,
music stores, museums and parks.
I am built to observe people,
stay objective, write things down.
I am built to appreciate Whitman but not live him.

See, I am not built to initiate walks or runs
outdoors or meet new people.
It was Kuma who pulled me to walk, to stroll,
to drop a towel, throw a ball.

It was Kuma who fidgeted behind my back on the beach,
jabbing and stabbing the warm sand to find his coolness,
staring like, "See? Now, you try it."

It was Kuma who forced me to laugh, to stroke
his chest, his legs, his paws. To feel the warm delight of
the sun, the joy of the air, the grace of the gulls.
The rhythm of the day, of the hour,
of the minute, of the second.
And I would breathe. I would close my eyes.
I would inhale and exhale. And breathe.
I still do.

That is Kuma.

January 5

In reading a compilation of *Paris Review* interviews tonight, the prolific novelist, Georges Simenon, mentions that "if a man has the urge to be an artist, it is because he needs to find himself. Every writer tries to find himself through his characters." This threw me across the room. Is this why I am so driven to walk, to journal, to jot down my every thought about you? The fear of losing you is one reason, but does your story subconsciously become a journey to find myself? After 64 years, I believe I know who I am, but if I keep writing, will I discover why your death hurts me so much? Why I don't want to shake this sense of unparalleled loss? Did you take me away from my life, or are you still leading me to a better way to live it? And why you?

January 7

My last semester of teaching. First day of class. First day of not rushing home from L.A. Fitness in order to walk you before it gets dark. First day of coming home from school to an empty house. First day of learning to live without someone who greeted me with instant love and gigantic goofiness when I opened the door. Who instinctually got excited to see me and felt joy every single time.

Doing our walk tonight, I felt extra lonely. Laughed to myself a few times thinking about you sniffing our front lawn right out of the gate. Also, when I passed some pee spots from your younger years, some from your older years, I envisioned your stance, your impassive demeanor. I fantasized about you coming back to me some day. It might be because as of 12/14, I stopped listening to my AirPods on our walks. I have more time to think. And feel.

January 9

Reading the LA Times this morning. A report about Ukraine Airlines Flight 752, a plane bound for Kiev was mysteriously shot down, killing 176 people. Hassan Shadkhoo, a Canadian citizen, upon hearing his wife died, told the CBC, "She was an angel . . . I wish I didn't exist right now." I jotted this down because it's exactly how I feel, like Mr. Shadkhoo's deep grief and loss was my own, but then it disturbed me to make such a comparison. A wife and a Kuma? How do I square this? Cause they aren't even close to being equal, but . . . I mean, I KNOW there isn't a true comparison between a human's life and an animal's life, but there must be something I'm missing here because I'm in some serious pain, severe darkness and unable to let you go.

January 10

Started shaking tonight. Uncontrollable trembling. Measured breathing kicked in. Didn't know if I was having a stroke so I dropped to the ground. Felt like your death just hit my body. Nothing like this since Rosie died 20 years ago. Rosie, my best friend from San Francisco, my unofficial guide to the city, moved to Belize to simplify her life. To live an authentic life. Around 1998, after living there for 5-6 years, she was brutally murdered. The following morning, as I was walking on the Pasadena City College campus headed to class, a friend from the Bay Area called to tell me of her death. My body froze. Felt my hands shaking, my breath tightening as a nearby city bus backfired, as horns blared, as fire engine sirens were rushing down Colorado Blvd. On campus, students were scrambling to their classes, on foot, bikes and skateboards, oblivious to the tragedy and for the first time in my life, I felt the world completely out of sync with life itself because it did not stop. The world did not stop. Would not pause. Spinning and spinning we all go like runaway tops. The insistence of life plows onward. So full of itself. Heartless, arrogant, sanctimonious, chillingly callous. I looked at the overcast skies, the only congruent piece of setting, and wailed, "FUCK! FUCK! FUCK!" I wanted God to hear me howl my anger and disdain, rejecting the failure of this existence. Someone so incredible, so important to so many, dies an ignoble death, and not a flinch, a nod, or an iota of acknowledgement. Again, I tremble.

January 13

Tomorrow will deliver the one-month anniversary of your death, and without the routine of bundling up in my Cotton On t-shirt, ratty blue sweater, and UCSC sweatshirt, without gathering your harness, leash, and poop bags, and without

The Blue Leash

my keys, iphone and NOLA baseball cap, I would be lost. Unmoored. The walk is all I know. We did it together more than 4,000 times, and now the walk has become my daily inspiration, my desert oasis, a charger for my inner sanctum. Since you left, I have an extra 45-60 minutes a day to do anything. I can binge watch a Netflix series; I can go grocery shopping, clean the kitchen floor, write belated Christmas cards, get a few beers at Lucky Baldwin's, a massage at HM Warm Spa, grade papers, bite my nails, learn piano, cook dinner, relearn the saxophone, repaint every room, take a bath instead of a shower. I could hit golf balls at the Altadena range every day of the week. There is so much to do that I don't want to do. The walk is all I know.

January 14

So, I'm going all the way up Michigan tonight as the sun yells out last call, but as I'm walking, I pass the baby palm you CONSTANTLY peed on, and I laugh disturbingly loud thinking how your ass would be dragging right about now. This steeper route going north? Those last few years you slowed down, pretending to be "observing" something, but it was obvious. Whenever you were engaged, your eyes were laser focused. Your weight would carry forward, not backwards. And you never would look at me until you're done. We hate to admit we're getting old, don't we?

Saddest part of tonight was when I tried to imagine you next to me, like I've been doing every day for weeks, and I couldn't do it. I couldn't fucking do it. Even the last few times I've walked, even last night, I could easily watch you trotting alongside me but not tonight. Easy to picture you strutting on the other side of the street from wherever I was, but I could not visualize you next to me tonight. My sense memory drew a blank. Is this when it happens? After only one month? I feel like a superhero losing his powers. What's next? Will I forget what you looked like? Does my heart turn to stone? Am I not allowed to feel a little joy during my sadness?

January 16

Traipsing the useless sidewalk to pick up the useless newspaper, before doing the same useless things in a Monday-Friday-with-weekends-off life. You are everywhere but here. These streets exist as nothing more than long, cavernous paths of vacuous energy. Look at them! Zombieville. Tonight a few people asked about your untethered leash - "My dog died a month ago, and I don't think I'm quite over it yet." Nod. Reel in the leash. Move along. One guy laughed? What's so funny? WHAT?

Last night, I dreamt about this dialogue by a river. Or an ocean. Late at night, pre-stormy, portentous clouds lined the moon's glow, pre-hurricane-ish, *Wizard of Oz*-like. I'm standing at the water's edge, discussing with a short, hatted stranger how I'm preparing to drown someone I love before they die. My rationale hinged on it's better to avoid the pain of waiting and watching them suffer. Loving is so hard. Letting go is so hard, but controlling the time and place makes it easier for everyone. The stranger looked at me kind of weird like I was speaking another language. I started walking into the water.

When I first heard my mom's cancer diagnosis out loud, I was in shock, like when a 5.8 earthquake rolled my house for ten seconds. Three months later, she was still alive, and all I felt was gratitude and hopefulness. Six months later, I was happily living my life adjusting to a new normal. Two years later, I was questioning how much longer is this going to go on? It dragged on much too long. The complete opposite of your death. So quick, so sudden. I am still struggling with these feelings of failure and impotence, of guilt for not being able to help you live longer. A month has gone by. What is a month? "By any other name . . . " When did a month feel this fast? Or this slow? I can't even tell what speed it was. Or is.

January 18

Part of my extreme love for you stems from sharing so much of our lives together for the past eleven years. We became our own universe, apart from any other relationship. We shared a life no one else was living. We had this unseen bond with a coded communication like the trees (as I just read in *The Overstory*) or the birds. Like being in a secret club with your neighborhood friends and all your parents are clueless. There was a special blend of traits. I became more chill; you became more adventurous. I talked more than ever; you tuned me out constantly. An understanding, a reading of each other's body language, heads turn, eyes touch, always in sync. Didn't need to be seen by anyone, or appreciated, or have our adventures posted on social media. It was just us. Just us doing us.

January 19

I see green. I see gray. Green yards and gray cement. Green bushes and gray driveways. Green leaves and gray tree trunks. Nature and sadness. New life and mourning. Youth and old age. Life and death.

Dismal cars cruise up and down Hill St., a tinge of blue cracking the gloominess above. The only life, the memory of my reddish-orange companion playing the foil for years to everything on this dead street. This historical plot of mythical orange groves gasps for meaning but finds nothing but exhausting, soundless engines and mowed sepulchers buried in sameness. I've spent years writing about surviving suicide, the dismantling of family, the dysfunction of education and watching the loss of a generation through the ubiquity of personal technology but nothing has ever, EVER hit me like losing my beautiful Kuma. I still don't know why. It's not that I don't want to be happy, or I enjoy playing the veiled widower in the village. I know I don't want another dog or another relationship that will obscure

The Blue Leash

my time with you. I'm still recalling and learning from it. How my voice, your leash, our postures, our language, all contributed to a sublime friendship through the years. I didn't appreciate it soon enough. I didn't see you were getting older. I could always see it in me but not you. I never thought of you as an age. More like an eternal flame.

BOOK II:
The Unexpected Path

"When someone you love dies, and you're not expecting it, you don't lose [them] all at once; you lose [them] in pieces over a long time – the way the mail stops coming, and [their] scent fades from the pillows . . . . Gradually, you accumulate the parts of [them] that are gone. Just when the day comes – when there's a particular missing part that overwhelms you with the feeling that [they're] gone, forever – there comes another day, and another specifically missing part."

– *A Prayer for Owen Meany*, John Irving

The Blue Leash

An Apple Falls

An apple falls.
The nurturing branch trembles.
The leaves sadly wave goodbye.
But the tree always cries.

An apple falls
So what?
Go get another one
They're all the same.

An apple falls
For over 10,000 years.
Colonists brought them here in the 1700s
Their colors vary, their flavors vary, their lives vary.
But their fates are all the same.

Scott D. DoVale

When an apple falls
Its gravitational potential energy converts to kinetic energy
If it doesn't bounce, its momentum is transferred to Earth
The combined momentum of the apple and the Earth
Leaves them both unchanged.
When an apple falls
The Earth moves toward the apple
The Earth and the apple move toward each other
With equal and oppositely directed momenta
The magnitude of the forces being equal.

The Earth moves toward the apple.

Why did the apple fall?
Did it naturally fall? Did it decide it was time to go?
What did the other apples think?
Did it inspire them? Scare them?
After all, the apples were growing up together, waiting to be picked.
They saw each other every day and then –

Nature breeds death.
Unexpectedly,
Like Dickinson's carriage driver, but much less cordial.
It plows over lives, uproots the temporal world, unearths frail realities, each time reminding every living thing of their own mortality.

The Blue Leash

And so we grieve. Read Didion.

Death breeds grief.
The ultimate sadness.
Every death affects our lives
Whether we're awake or asleep
but not every death makes us grieve.
We grieve because we shared love. Read C. S. Lewis.
We shared time. We shared space. Read Donne.
We shared hearts. We shared souls. Read *Annabel Lee*.
And so, we grieve our own death.

Grief breeds mourning.
Mourning expresses grief outwardly.
Not only with black veils and arm bands.
Not only with funerals and candles.
Or hyacinth, or flags at half-mast
Or getting drunk. Or posting on social media.

Mourning can be tears and screams,
trembling and aching,
losing breath, losing hope,
talking and sharing and dispelling pain.
But grief does not always breed mourning.

We allow ourselves to mourn, or maybe we don't.
We allow others to mourn, or maybe we won't.

Scott D. DoVale

Because we are taught how to grieve.
What our family does, what our religion does.
What is proper etiquette and what is not.
What is acceptable and what is not.
What is inappropriate, unsuitable, tasteless, indulgent, excessive, weak . . .
And what is not.

But when a soul grieves, it needs to mourn.
The pain must be expelled.
Merciless, relentless, mortally wounding loss must be expelled.

I miss my apple.

The Blue Leash

10 Things I Miss about Kuma:
1. His expressive, brown eyes
2. His gumdrop, black nose
3. His supine, sublime posing
4. His wickedly handsome smile
5. His wiggly, martini-shaped ass
6. His spinning for breakfast
7. His sense of independence (did I say adamant?)
8. His regal, bouncy gait
9. His attention-getting handsomeness
10. His crescent-shaped, multi-linguistic tail
11. His unwavering focus when catching flies
12. When he flies . . .

The Blue Leash

A Rise to Prominence

How can one describe a miracle if one has never witnessed one? In trying to explain the unexplainable, Evel Knievel jumps to mind, leaping over 14 busses on his motorcycle at Caesar's Palace. A chained Houdini escaping from a Chinese water torture cell on Halloween night (at least in the movie starring Tony Curtis). The local reporter from the Pasadena Star News compared the following unexplainable event to the Texas Longhorns' upset of USC in the 2006 Rose Bowl. Even the Los Angeles Times referenced the 1980 Miracle on Ice as a marking point. But for most of the people who live here, it was nothing less than a divine miracle bestowed on them as an existential blessing. Or a harbinger of the apocalypse. Either way, Maddy Headstrong witnessed it and will never see the world quite the same.

Scott D. DoVale

For Maddy it was a normal day. Sunny, quiet, normal day. A normal day inside of a normal week inside of a normal year. Like a temporal turducken. Except this was not a normal day. It was March 23, 2010. Maddy, dressed in a green-patterned maxi, yellow sash and possibly the first pair of Birkenstocks ever made in the United States, had woken with an Irish smile and an Ivory soft complexion to greet the day. She did everything earlier than usual – performed her yoga, fed the chickens, drank her soy protein shake, read the community newsletter – all because today was her birthday party for Sammy D., her one-eyed beagle boy. Oh, how she loved him so and nothing was going to interfere with her birthday party for Sammy D. Actually, it wasn't exactly a birthday party but more of a playdate. Well, it was kind of a combination of the two because a party needs to have . . . oh, forget it, let her tell the story:

"As the narrator just said, I woke up extra early all so excited to decorate for Sammy's birthday party. I did my normal routine. I also picked up the poop in the backyard, and then I strung twisted pink and white crepe paper streamers across the living room ceiling, tied a dozen pink balloons to the dining room chairs, set up snack dishes with mini-bacon bones in the dining room, vegetarian biscuits near the zucchini garden and prepared her favorite meal for the party

The Blue Leash

– roasted chicken with bacon. This was my first time hosting a party for Sammy D., and I wanted it to be very special.

See, Sammy's a rescue. She's eight years old and all she's ever done is make puppies in a puppy mill. People can be so damn evil! We got her almost a year ago, and all she does is stay in her crate in the spare bedroom. When she does go out, she runs around in circles in the backyard. If you went out there now, you'd see it looks like a motor cross raceway. But that's ok. And her eye? I have no idea how that happened except people suck. Did I say that already? But she's got a good heart. So, this day was a very big deal for both of us. I never had another dog over because I didn't know how she would react, or if she'd even come out of her crate.

See, this all started a few weeks ago. Sammy D. and I were walking around Bungalow Heaven, which was a weird thing in itself because she doesn't like to go for walks, but I wanted her to get some fresh air and socialize a bit and so we're walking over on Holliston, and Sammy D. starts darting along really quick, like she's scared of something, like she's going to get mugged. I always think she's from New York. So, I keep pulling her leash back so I can look at my neighborhood more, you know, see all the beautiful homes and gardens. People really put *so much work into their yards. Like the Downings! They just finished constructing a stone waterfall in the front with water lilies and koi fish. Who thinks of these things? All we've got is Frankie, my plastic, pink flamingo. Anyway, we're walking and I stopped to look at my phone, but Sammy D. didn't want to stop. She puts her little head down and tries to pull me like The Tiny Motor that Could. You know, the book? She finally pulls over and starts smelling this bush with these purple flowers and Moroccan-like leaves when I see a man walking towards us with his dog. It was Scott and Kuma. Well, Sammy went gaga over this beautiful dog, this - I'd never seen this type of dog before. Very majestic, like a groomed wolf, and yet pretty approachable, you know? He stared at me like the principal at my old high school! Sammy's tail is wagging, her head is bouncing and she walks right up to Kuma, smells his "down under" and starts licking his ears and his face. I never saw her do anything like that before. Any time we ever meet a dog, she shrivels like a little raisin, or she races to the curb pretending she has to pee. I mean it was strange, in a good way strange, and Kuma just stood there, like this happens to him all the time. Like he was used to dogs adoring him. I thought, you know, if this is what makes Sammy happy. I never did this before, but I asked Scott if he'd be*

The Blue Leash

interested in having a playdate for Kuma someday. So, we exchanged phone numbers and by the time we got home, I got the idea for Sammy's birthday party/playdate, called Scott and invited Kuma over for the following week. I said it was Sammy D.'s birthday. I thought it would make it sound more important, but we don't really know her birthday cause she's a rescue.

So, the party was on a Friday. It was right around 12:30 when I dragged Sammy D. out of her crate, dressed her in a Jerry Garcia tie dye shirt that read, "Birthday Girl," put a nice, pink bow on her head, and misted her with a bit of Fifi perfume. Scott brought Kuma over around 1. He wasn't dressed at all. Kuma, I mean. Not that I expected him to be, but Sammy D. looked a bit overdressed so I put a bandana around Kuma's neck after Scott left just to liven up the party a bit.

Scott seemed a bit nervous leaving him. He kept telling me Kuma was only a year old and this was his first playdate and Shibas were runners and he only takes Kuma outside on a leash or in their fenced backyard. Blah, blah, blah. A bit too paranoid if you ask me, but he was a first-time parent. He never owned a dog before so I kind of understood. I told him Bill and I have had seven or eight dogs so he didn't need to worry. I'd watch Kuma the whole time. Keep them both in the house or backyard together and after about five minutes of telling Kuma how much he loved him and he'll be fine and have lots of fun and be a good boy, Scott finally left.

So, as soon as I shut the door, Sammy D. came running out of her crate like there was an earthquake and headed straight down the hall to Kuma. She NEVER left the crate before for anyone! I swear it was a miracle! I put 101 Dalmatians on the TV. They started eating their snacks right away. I remember Kuma taking one of Sammy's rawhide bones and being like pretty chill with it, gnawing it under the dining room table. Sammy sat next to him, adoring him like she was in love, watching him eat her favorite bone. Everything was going fan-TAS-ti-cally! No drama whatsoever. So, I went in the back to do some laundry. Then my sister called about whose turn it was to walk Mom around the park. Didn't talk too long, maybe 2-3 minutes, and then I went back to the dining room to get the kids so they could run around outside. I had set up a little obstacle course in the backyard and well, I see Sammy standing at the front door staring out. I remember thinking she looked like Lazarus when Jesus raised him from the dead. The sun was really bright, shining through the doorway, and her silhouette – anyway, I went to grab my phone to take a picture and then I just stopped. Sammy's bone was under the table all by itself. The front door was wide open! I froze for a few seconds and then ran outside and called Kuma's name up and down the sidewalk. Nothing. I didn't want to call Scott right away because I knew he would freak out. I searched through each room in the house, the backyard, the obstacle course, the back of the pickup. I looked under the rug and behind the shower curtain. I even looked in the toilet. You know how you look in the refrigerator sometimes when you're missing your keys? I ended up back in the living room, and Sammy D. was still at the front door looking out. She kinda twisted her neck around and looked at me with the saddest eyes, like, 'Mom, Kuma ran away.' Finally, I called Scott. Told him Kuma might be missing.

So, not sure what happened after that. I mean I know what happened. I walked out the front door. Scott got here quicker than a jack rabbit on his hutch mate. He was running down the street yelling Kuma's name. We searched my house again, and eventually Scott ran over to McDonald's Park, which is where we all bring our dogs. It's about three blocks away. I felt absolutely terrible. I'm standing on the sidewalk in front of my house, tearing up, feeling totally guilty. I was scared something bad might happen. You know, maybe he'll get hit by a car. Maybe a coyote will find him and eat him. People are constantly losing their cats and dogs here to coyotes. Then I thought maybe someone saw him in the doorway and abducted him. I mean he is such a drop dead, handsome dog. The other day I read how some woman in Malibu walked into a house and stole a baby so if it can happen there, right?

So, there I am, pretty nervous, very distraught, when this warm breeze starts sweeping through my hair, tingling my head, down my neck, a little on my shoulders. Like a spirit was touching me or something. I instinctively dropped down, went into the chin mudra position, closed my eyes, and began to center myself. Took a few deep breaths and slowly I began to feel this incredible calm, this sense like everything was going to be ok. Kuma was going to be ok. I was going to be ok. So, after another minute or so, I opened my eyes, looked up to the sky to thank God and there he was! Kuma! There was Kuma! The fucking dog was floating right above me! 'Scuse my language but he was flying over my house! Above the wires and the tree tops. He was like a small blimp, like a Goodyear stuffed animal. He wasn't quite hovering, but he was drifting r-e-a-l slow. I fucking screamed, "Kuma!" Sorry, again. And he was fine. He looked pretty happy, peaceful, like he flies all the time. Then Sally Castro comes out of her house cause I screamed, and I'm pointing and she looks up and says, "What the fu . . . fudge!" And then

The Blue Leash

at least another six or seven other neighbors come out while Kuma's blimping away from us, heading towards Michigan Ave. over the Kennedy's house and over the Finkle's house, maneuvering around a few oak trees and telephone poles. We all started walking pretty fast up the street trying to follow his path and I'm jogging a bit and I totally left my door open and forgot about Sammy but I mean everyone was like hypnotized like we all drank the same Kool-Aid and we all hurried over to the next street and this is the part I will never forget although I won't forget any of it until the day the Lord takes me but just as I got over to the next street I'm within maybe four houses of Scott's and there's Kuma coming down real gently like Mary Poppins – just like freakin' Mary Poppins – and he comes down and barely misses the roof of his house and ends up landing perfectly in the middle of his front porch. I would say I was nuts if I was the only one who saw him, but it was real. It happened. Kuma actually flew home. He flew! And I'm really good at detecting things, you know, like CSI or Columbo, figuring things out, and I swear I saw these small wings come out from under his fur. Mary Vlaanderen said she saw it. Jack next door says he didn't see it, but his wife, Sally, definitely did, and Peter said he might have seen like dove's wings pop out. A-mazzzz-ing!

Anyway, Kuma sat there like nothing happened, looking at everyone and smiling. His aura was beaming a radiant purple, which is the highest of all chakra colors. It sent chills, goosebumps, over my arms and legs. There were maybe twenty of us standing on the sidewalk – smiling, laughing, stunned – pretty much speechless. The topper was when he began to yodel. I think he was calling his ancestors. It was Call of the Wild meets Pasadena.

Of course, then I started crying. I don't know if I cried because the whole thing was so magical or supernatural or because he was okay and I wasn't responsible for his death, which easily could have happened because aside from coyotes, we have a neighborhood of racecar drivers around here. But I was crying and then I feel this big smile comes over my face. I witnessed something amazing, something spiritual, like maybe only fifteen or twenty people witnessed on the entire planet. I felt like I was chosen to see this for a reason. Like my life had a real purpose.

I eventually called Scott. As soon as he got home, he ran up the porch. Kuma started wagging his tail, doing pirouettes, front legs popping like a low rider down Colorado, and Scott started hugging him so tight for so long. The love he felt for Kuma! You could touch it. The weirdest part, even though a dog flying is like the weirdest part, but after Scott stood up, I was standing right in front of the porch, and he came down and asked me how I found Kuma.

"Didn't you see him?"

"No, I was running around screaming his name for ten blocks. Where did you find him?"

I told him I saw him up in the sky flying, and I followed him until he landed on the porch. That's why all his neighbors were standing around his house. He didn't believe me. Other people chimed in but Scott refused to believe us. I think he thought we were mocking him or something, but he thanked me, thanked our neighbors, and right before Scott brought Kuma into the house, Kuma gave me a stare to thank me as well and right then, I felt this sense of peace within myself, like everything was as it should be. Then he turned and walked into the house.

The next day the Pasadena Star News ran the story on the front page, bottom right-hand corner. They titled it, "Was that a Flying Dog?" as if there was any question! They interviewed me and the neighbors, even people who swore they saw him from a half mile away. The police had been called while he was flying, but they thought it was fake news. Some people thought Kuma was a big kite or a government drone. I don't know if Scott saw the article. We don't talk much. The courteous "Hi," but he's definitely holding a grudge, like it was my fault that Kuma got away. I mean it was, but . . . he told me Kuma was a runner, but he didn't say he was a flyer. All I know is it was the greatest day of my life."

Maddy Headstrong witnessed a supernatural event, a flight of fancy, without any rational explanation, but Kuma's magical mystery tour inspired her to adopt his Japanese ancestry. She built a small shrine in her bedroom, devoting herself to the Shinto tenets of cleanliness, cheerfulness, and harmony with Nature. For the next few months, she had dreams of Kuma flying over the Vatican and the Buddhist temples in Tibet. His image sometimes morphed into Pegasus; other times he was a psychiatrist talking to Maddy about her life while she was lying on a sofa. After months of having her eyewitness account questioned, Maddy arranged to take a polygraph test at the Pasadena police station. Of course, she passed with "flying Kumas," and shared her glowing results on the neighborhood app with an inappropriate GIF that soon had her free membership cancelled.

As for Scott, it took him months to accept Kuma's aerial feat. He had read all the articles and watched the local news coverage, but who could trust the media these days? And what about Rolling Stone's interview with Kuma? That had to be fiction, right? I mean they did come to his house and sit with Kuma for hours, but it all felt a bit too much, like

The Blue Leash

a Twilight Zone episode. He thought Maddy made up the story because her life was so normal and boring. If Shibas are known to run away, why would Kuma fly back home? And why didn't Kuma ever fly for him? He never got over the fact that Maddy almost lost Kuma. He also never got over the fact that he almost lost Kuma.

As for Kuma, he never left the house again without a leash, and he never experienced another playdate. But he did experience flight, my dear canine lovers, and that made him extremely well-known, well-loved and very hungry, my dear friends, very hungry!

*"The deepest of communication is not
communication but communion. It is wordless . . .
beyond speech . . . beyond concept."*
– T. Merton

The Blue Leash

The Sounds of Shiba Silence

Paradise exists 90 miles north of Los Angeles. The tallest palm trees. Cerulean blue ocean. Delicious range mountains. As long as paradise includes Mediterranean temperatures, beautiful beaches, great food, wine, micro-breweries, and activities up the wazoo, including a zoo, then Santa Barbara qualifies as a Genesis-inspired haven. Minus original sin. A perfect retreat for those weary of heart and spirit. Leaving behind anxieties, house chores, and emails, comfortably cruising the last fifteen miles, winding through Carpinteria ... Summerland ... Montecito ... peering at the coastline ... breathing in the fresh, crisp air ... it changes you. Makes you believe there are still different rhythms and patterns to live your life by. That you can control your little piece of the world. That there are alternate endings if one can dream them. That you still have choices to reinvigorate, resuscitate, and even reinvent your one and only life here on Earth.

With that in mind, every New Year's and Fourth of July, Kuma retreats to the Santa Barbara Inn to examine his one life. Well, he also helps Scott and his family recalibrate their lives, but Kuma gets a chance to get off the hamster wheel and find peace away from the cats and the mailman. In fact, before his crate ever leaves the car's trunk, Kuma races into the hotel room and enthrones himself on the bed closest to the ocean-view window. Once his family concedes, he jumps down and inspects the room's perimeter with FBI-caliber sniffing of the bedrooms, bathrooms, closets and carpets, mixing in a few feigned leg-lifts on the you-name-the-furniture until Scott yells his name in protest. Kuma loves to make the family laugh, but he also knows it's his duty to alert them of any nasty remnants found in their hotel room.

"Do they know this hotel allows chihuahuas with fleas? Or the towel's scent includes rodent spray, or the room's air conditioner circulates dust mites and mildew allergens which is why the kids sneeze so much? Have to tell Scott - wait! Pepperoni pizza under the bed? Whoa, not a bad hotel!"

Surrounded by palms, tourists and a growing homeless population, Kuma's family begins each morning with the lobby breakfast, fitness center and Kuma's walk to Pirate's Cove. Daily activities range from touring the Channel Islands and sailing

The Blue Leash

among a pod of dolphins to kayaking, paddle boarding, or shooting pool at Mr. Q's. In the afternoon, the family morphs into Butterfly Beach-ed whales or lounging lizards by the pool but whatever tetrapod they choose to be, dinners are always the day's pièce de résistance! Kuma and his family exist for food. The Palace, The Lark, Night Lizard Brewing, Original Joe's. Doesn't matter. And they always end with a ritualistic demolition of the most indulgent dessert on the menu. They eat like piranhas, laugh like hyenas and reminisce like a herd of elephants? And always with Kuma. And always a phenomenal experience. And always a special time of bonding. Always. Twice a year for the last 15 years. Always nirvana. Always. Without exception!

Except this one year.

Driving up the 101, winding through four lanes of bumper-to-bumper traffic like a caffeinated caterpillar, Kuma's family wasn't half way to Eden before the back seat erupted. Girl pushed boy, boy pushed back, Kuma stirred, mom checked her emails, dad shifted in the driver's seat. Girl pushed boy harder, boy raised a fist, Kuma yawned, "Time out," Mom said, "Enough," boy yelled, "Don't," girl wailed gender discrimination, foul words were volleyed like ping pong balls, until Dad glared into the adjusted mirror and barked, "SHUT THE FUCK UP! Do you want me to turn around and go home? I'm trying to drive! Kuma's trying to sleep! So, shut the fuck UP!" Kuma groaned. This was the first time Scott ever dropped the "F" bomb in front of the kids. And the second time. For the next 40 miles, the car maintained a disturbing silence infused with frustration, anger and resentment. Eventually, lips murmured but for the most part of the next two days, they were four mimes acting in a silent film. The magical mystery tour did not appear in the summer of 2015.

On the second morning of mumbling, while the mimes split up the eggs, bagels, fresh fruit, and coffee, Kuma consumed the awkward tension in the room. They all acted like boarded dogs with dysfunctional noses. Or like wounded animals wary of being touched. The silence interrupted only by shuffling feet, slammed dresser drawers and the obligatory "Excuse me" as they passed one another. Not sensing a detente, and seconds away from all of them dispersing for biking, paddle boarding, shopping and Mr. Q's bar and grill, Kuma rose from his Sealy King throne and emitted his high-pitched Shiba yodel, culminating with his black eyes piercing through Scott, who resigned himself to no one visibly listening. "I guess I'm taking care of Kuma today." He grabbed the leash, the poop bag dispenser, his journal and a few books. He hooked Kuma's collar and hustled out the door, leaving the hotel room and his family behind.

Kuma shifted into alpha mode, directing Scott through the parking lot's labyrinth and straight to his favorite strip of lawn. Not only did the neighboring Motel 6 offer him a perfect place for morning doo and a local message board for visiting dogs, but the Bermuda grass gave him a supple atmosphere for thinking. Today was only going to be a rerun of yesterday, ending in more tension, sarcasm and no dessert. Kuma knew Scott went too far this time, and now

The Blue Leash

that he's got him alone, how can he sway him to admit his mistake and apologize to the family? They only had two more nights, and they hadn't even gone to the ocean yet. The ocean!

After peeing and pawing the lemon-drop lawn like a baby bull, Kuma yanked Scott's arm and led him directly to the beach. He knew how Scott lived and breathed the ocean. He knew the meditative shoreline along Cabrillo provided a sanctuary for Scott to be alone with Kuma, his journal and his thoughts. Deftly avoiding run amok kids and the roller-skating mariachi, they reached the crowded strand, as Kuma abruptly stopped in the middle of the bike path. He took a few steps towards the ocean, as if Neptune was willing him to come closer, and pretended to be observing the pelicans, but he knew sitting on the beach right now would give Scott a chance to see things more -

"Why are you stopping here? I thought you didn't like the beach? Did you bring a towel because I didn't bring one?"

Kuma stared at him. "You love the beach. Right? This is your favorite spot. Right? This is where you think. Right?"

"Sure, let's do what you want. This whole weekend is shot, anyway. Can't take you to Mr. Q's so why not?"

On the back of the berm, while the sunlight peeked through the clouds, Kuma chose a shady refuge away from the chattering multitude of early beachgoers. He curled on the sand and feigned sleep, as he monitored Scott losing himself again in his 15th reading of *The Scarlet Letter*.

Kuma hoped Hawthorne's counsel might prod his friend to resolve the family impasse very soon because Kuma despised conflicts; they increased his anxiety and prolonged his Apoquil prescription. After about an hour, intermittently sniffing the grilled burgers, dried algae, coconut tanning lotion, BBQ sauce, and Wild Turkey, Kuma could still smell Scott's salty sullenness. Normally, Scott's escape into the Puritan classic led him to the public scaffold of guilt and repentance; instead, he drifted closer to an island of self-righteous indignation.

"But this is the ocean," Kuma thought, "It should give him the answer."

Any other time, Kuma's ears would be peaked listening to Scott recreation of his "famed" lecture on Emerson and Thoreau. Bringing up the Transcendentalist's belief that under natural environs a person can find their own truth, Scott dramatically encouraged his new batch of juniors each year to transcend school and transport themselves to the Pacific. He repeated the lesson annually on the beach for the family's edification and approval.

"So, let's say you're at Santa Monica beach. By yourself. Without your phone."

The class laughed, groaned and yelled, "Never!"

"Use your imagination! You're far away from the pier. It's very peaceful. You hear the rhythmic crash of the waves, the mewing of a couple dozen seagulls. No one else is around. Just you. What do you smell?"

The Blue Leash

"The salt in the air!"

"Hot dogs!"

"Popcorn?"

"OK, and when you look up and down the coast, and you look out at the horizon, what do you see?

"The ocean?"

"Thank you, Mr. Obvious. And what do you notice about the ocean?"

"How big it is?"

"Great. A different perspective! Good. Context. What else?"

"The horizon looks forever. Like infinite."

"Right. Great! And then what might you start thinking about?"

And after a few comments about gull turds and being hungry -

"Your life?"

"Exactly! Well, not my life but yours! Yes, your life in relationship to the world. How small your world is, how minuscule your problems are compared to this incredible, breathtaking vastness. And then, maybe, you might think what is your purpose? Why are you here?"

Kuma loved this lecture. He would picture himself in Scott's class with his eyes closed, thinking about the giant ocean, growing up in his Oregon home with his family along the coast. His dad's stories about Kit and the origin of Shibas, and how Keri brought him this new life with Scott and his family. A tear of gratitude would softly drop, like the Times Square Ball on New Year's, as the lecture's inspiration naturally reaffirmed Kuma's true purpose. Unfortunately, Scott was not rekindling the lecture or his own true purpose today.

"I can't believe they're not talking to me. I almost hit that semi with all that stupid, freaking noise in the car, and Melissa sitting on her phone, not doing a damn thing and everyone is acting like I'm the bad guy. 'Oh, Dad said fuck.' Yeah, I'm so terrible. Fuck that. Oops, said it again!"

A transient, Nick Nolte doppelgänger emerged from the glaring sunlight.

"Excuse me. Do you have any change? Anything would help. Nice dog."

"I don't have any money with me. Sorry."

Kuma scowled. Stared. He raised his right paw towards Scott's pocket.

"Wait a second." Scott pulled out a ten. "I forgot I brought my wallet."

"That's very kind. Not too many people here like you. Gorgeous dog. Have a great day."

Whenever Scott experienced anything reminiscent of his childhood heartbreak - *(HIS PARENT'S DIVORCE)* - he got overwhelmed and retreated into his shell. *Kuma touched his cheek with his nose.* All the same feelings of detachment, of loud voices accusing and echoing. *Kuma laid next to him upside-down.* How there was no stability, no one to turn to anymore. The silence seeped tension into his veins. *Kuma tried to make a sand angel.* Scott glanced at Kuma, smiled, and closed his eyes, mooring himself next to the harbor's yachts.

Obviously, the whole transcendent idea backfired so Kuma pressed his 35 lb. heft against Scott's back, and nudged him off his sandy throne. He jumped up, barked at the gulls, and ran around in circles. The universe pitched in with the harbor boats honking, the gulls inching closer and the unsupervised children even closer. And louder! Scott closed his book.

"What? What are you doing? Let me guess. You're bored and want to go somewhere else?"

Kuma HOWLED like Ginsberg. "SCOTT, IT'S TIME TO MOVE!" The canine poet grinned.

"What was that? Are you in pain? Where do you want to go?"

Kuma moved like Jaggar, blue-steeled like Derek Zoolander. "Trust me."

Challenging his restraint, Kuma pulled Scott in a new direction, away from the impotent ocean to a more fertile intoxication. Weaving through local bladers, tourists, surreys, runners, walkers, and every other human impediment, Kuma's inspired pace recalled the swift, dexterous moves of Buck from "The Call of the Wild," except for his increased panting and his chest heaving as he passed by West Beach, his favorite place for startling gulls and exploring tide pool anemones. Kuma's view of the world might stand only eighteen inches tall, but his love and devotion for Scott towered over his own desires and limitations, as well as the city's contrived holiday streetlights and synchronized palms.

The trek, from the salty strand to the trendy main street of commerce, led Kuma towards the dark underpass. A bewildering stretch strewn with famished grocery carts, deceased blankets and broken hearts laying in the shadows. Weathered faces emerged and brightened as he passed, wanting to say hello and asking if they can "pet your dog." It confused Kuma why there were people living in paradise like stray dogs. With his eyes opening wider, while dodging the careless gait of sandaled feet and perfumed legs, Kuma's nose instinctively refocused on ferreting out the potent scents of whiskey and dark roast. Passing several massage parlors, a smoke shop, and a litter of dying businesses, Kuma entered the more successful blocks of State Street. Within minutes, he victoriously arrived at the hallowed entrance to the open-bricked, stale beer smelling pantheon of drink. *The James Joyce*. A dank, crusty, Guinness-pouring, dart throwing, Irish pub. A black hole of libations oblivious to the neighboring scrim of retro boutiques, chic restaurants, and corporate chains. *Scott laughed, looked down at Kuma and walked in, leaving an ounce of his melancholy on the sidewalk.* Kuma strutted in behind him. *A laugh!*

The musty bar's familiar odors - the crushed peanut shells, forgotten cigarettes, ancient hops, and the sole

The Blue Leash

customer's rank emanating off the barstool, along with the collective breath of whiskey and stout, permeated the barroom and crept into Kuma's nose. Scott ordered at the bar while Kuma settled at a wooden table in the front. The coconut-flavored cocktail waitress came over, offering a bowl of cool water.

"Aren't you a handsome one? Here, let me open the window for you."

Kuma jumped up on the seat to look out while she set his water on the table.

Scott sat down embracing his Irish coffee.

"You have a gorgeous dog. He acts like he's human."

"Sometimes I think he is. Thank you." She walked away.

"Don't say it."

Kuma said nothing; he stared back only to relish Scott's first grin of the day. Maybe it was Van Morrison wailing on the jukebox, or the pungent air loitering from years of drunken festivities. The austere emptiness. The wooden solitude. The Irish coffee. *"We were born before the wind / Also, younger than the sun."* All Kuma knew was whenever his best friend came here, he ended up happy. Most of the time Scott reset himself at the beach - rekindling his state of mind, his purpose, and embracing his role as "Summer Daddy." But whenever the seashore lost its mojo . . .

"Here, have a sip." Kuma licked the whipped cream.

Twenty minutes passed. Scott tested his second Irish, looked out the window and watched families being families.

Sharing Cold Stone cups. Taking pictures near the dolphin statue. Parents holding hands while their kids beheld the street's liveliness, their innocent laughter piercing through his heart. He looked at Kuma who looked right back.

"I just wanted everything perfect. That's why we come here. Great weather. Great food. Drinks! The ocean. Not too many people. And I know the universe doesn't care what I want. *(Pause)* I hate when this shit happens. It's like being in a car wreck. I see it coming, but I just close my eyes and wait for the impact. Then everything gets eerily quiet. You see Mom's face this morning? The kids hate me. Sometimes I can be a real asshole. I should wear an A on my chest like Hester."

Kuma softened his stare. "I love you."

His eyes panned out to the street of humans, of many ages, colors and stories. His golden muzzle stretched and sniffed, investing in the joys and fears of everyone who passed by. The town offered a restless tone, a more disparate blend of haves and have nots than at home. He listened to the raucous mingling of voices, the inebriated shouts from sports bars. Still unable to shake the swollen faces, the gentler souls, withering while so many looked the other way. Like they were lampposts or fire hydrants.

Scott cleared his throat.

"You see all the homeless on our way over here? It's so sad."

The scales on Scott's eyes were starting to fall. A tanned, blonde, 20-something did a double-take and stopped to pay homage.

The Blue Leash

"Is he a Shiba? OMG! He is so cute! What's his name?"

"Kuma."

"Kuma, you are amazing! Can I pet you?"

"He tends to bite strangers."

"Dogs love me." She pet him and took a selfie. "Have a great day!"

Scott shook his head. "What is it with you? People cross the street to see you. I mean, you're charming and all that. Great smile but . . ."

An older woman stopped in her roller skating tracks, regained her balance and visually took in Kuma's framed face like a painting at the Louvre. Her broadening smile barely contained her whitened teeth.

"I've never seen such a distinguished dog. Does he always sit at the table with you?"

"No, sometimes I sit on the floor."

"My family had a Shiba for years. Foxy Roxy. A little thinner. Had a blue aura. But your dog's energy is so pure."

"Kuma has an aura?"

"You can't see it? It's white as snow with light, violet sparkles."

"Where is Foxy Roxy?"

"He died. They do that unfortunately."

"Yeah, well, Kuma's going to outlive me so . . ."

"Are you and Kuma visiting?"

"Yes, we are. We're having a men's day today. Doing what men do."

"Well, this bar's a little too depressing for me. I'm going to the Oyster House. I'll buy Kuma a drink if you guys stop by."

Needless to say, Kuma owned people. He could be one of the great wingmen of all time. His presence invited attention and shunned validation. Swirling, thick fur of orange with eyes born centuries ago. He never flaunted his import with an exaggerated swagger or a commanding gait. He only knew how to be himself. Even as they left the *James Joyce*, the homeless veteran's dog on the corner of Cota and State bowed and offered his soiled sniff to Kuma.

"He doesn't bite. He just wants to smell your dog. Handsome."

"So, I'm told. Thank you. And yours is -"

"Hungry. That's his name, too. Don't know what I'd do without him."

"Yeah. Me, too." He handed the man five dollars. Then handed him a twenty.

"God bless you, sir!"

Six blocks went by as Kuma steered Scott to an era gone by that never really left. A forgotten path, a slower pace, he created some slack on his leash to let Scott feel like he was in control. Scott looked at his watch.

"Maybe we should head back to the hotel. Or maybe I should call Melissa to tell her where we are. She probably doesn't care at this point but I don't know what to do."

Kuma hung his fang out as they turned the corner, unleashing his final destination.

The Blue Leash

An old, stucco Italian restaurant, with a tiled patio of young Americans adulting, stylishly old Europeans blending, along with a few retired locals, all sipping reds and whites, feasting on olive-crusted this and basil-infused that. Festive sounds, clinking chatter, romantic tongues under a string of resilient white lights.

"I don't need another drink. OK, maybe I do."

Kuma scrunched up his eyes at Scott. "Seriously? Don't you remember?"

"You want pizza?"

Kuma shook his head and looked down. He couldn't believe it, but Scott was getting old.

"Oh, now I remember! 'Table for five, please.' Your first restaurant! We sat right over there. What a disaster! Kate spilled my Sam Adams. Max threw up his spaghetti. And you rained on that potted plant!" *The elusive smile.* "Mom and I snatched napkins off the tables, got paper towels from the bar. You started slurping up the spaghetti, your nose smeared in tomato sauce. You were so cute!" *The second laugh.*

Kuma pretended not to hear him. He sat on the sidewalk, licking his inner thigh, but that was it! Something about the "accidents" of life, the unscripted moments, that become so important, so memorable. Kuma knew that. He knew that from the day he was born.

"The waiter, tall guy with a mohawk, and the owner, Mr. Pascucci. So gracious! We sat back down, finished our dinner! The staff took a picture with you. Great night! Great night. And I remember I didn't get mad. I didn't yell. I just loved being..."

Kuma witnessed the proverbial light going off in Scott's head.

Scott suddenly realized what eluded him for the past two days. Maybe he took on the worn clothes of his father. Possibly his father's father. Swearing and overreacting. Coming down too heavy, too quick. But being a dad was all he lived for and he cared so much and wanted to be the best father and he wanted to help his kids avoid the mistakes and make better choices and believe in themselves like he never did and...

"Hey, is that Kuma?"

"Mr. Pascucci?"

"Yes! I remember him from when? Maybe 4, 5 years ago?"

"Might be. Place still looks great."

"Thank you. My son took over a few years ago. Him and his wife picked up the business quite a bit. Wifi, food deliveries, wine flights. Microbrews? It does a father good. How's Kuma? Such a prince. I still have his picture with the staff behind the bar. You're very lucky."

Time. The existential tsunami. Hardly noticeable, maybe a rumble or two in your 30s and then around 50 or so, it rushes up and boom! Red licorice loses to cavities. Potentials cede to necessities. Dreamers to dream makers. Hopefully. And the exuberance of sibling fights and spontaneous yelling become . . . well, we become our fathers and mothers. Much too soon.

"Mr. Pascucci. Can we get a reservation for dinner? Maybe around 7?

"Table for five? I remember!"

Kuma brushed against the owner. "Table for five!"

"Let's go, Kuma. I need to apologize to the troops. Summer Daddy just arrived."

State Street served as a parade route for Kuma's bandleading tail. The sad stores more exotic and daring. Gift shops, crowded with t-shirts, key rings and shot glasses, transformed back into "quaint," and Santa Barbara's main street sparked fond memories once again. But Kuma knew it wasn't a paradise. No place can be a paradise. *Paradise is waiting back at the hotel.*

"Hey! Wait a second." Scott pulled Kuma to a standstill. He got down on one knee and kissed Kuma's forehead. Tears planted in the princely fur. "Thank you."

Kuma cried, too. He had cried before but this was different. He had cried when Scott stopped talking to him because he ate the cat's food. The day Grandma died. When the family boarded him for two weeks before their trip to Paris. No, these were tears of joy. The other kind made his whole face fall down. This time his face rose up.

Kuma never forgot the summer of 2015.

> *"Grief is like living two lives.
> One is where you pretend that everything is alright,
> and the other is where your heart silently screams in pain."*
> — **Unknown**

The Blue Leash

Before opening the front door, Ed tightens the drapes, thwarting the sun from warming his bungalow's living room and brightening the dim, mission-style furniture. He toggles the coffee maker, puts on his baseball cap, grabs his cane and peers through the door's window before hobbling down to the end of the driveway. He slowly bends over to pick up the newspaper.

E – Damn it!

The driveway's dried pine needles pierce his socks once again! And then there's Rich, his neighbor across the tree-lined street, always lurking on his porch, waiting to talk to anybody.

R – "Good morning, Ed! Beautiful day today!"

Ed turns back up the driveway, waves.

E – *(Muttering)* – If you're a squirrel! It's just another stupid day. Which is fine. Never mind the virus. The stock market. The damn protesters. What a shitshow.

The greens and blues escape Ed's attention again as he locks himself back into his century old fortress. It's Monday. The dreary coffee maker beeps as he pulls up his untethered red, white and blue pajamas. The cold, granite kitchen floor brings relief to his encrusted feet as he shuffles over to the wooden cabinet to get his 1988 Dodgers World Champions cup, and then he opens the fridge.

E – Soy cream? What happened to cream cream?

Standing at the sink, he pours the coffee, adds the soy, three cubes of sugar, and stirs. He scans the newspaper, shifting his view from one minute to the next. The left is too this; the right is always that, and then onto the –

E – There's no sports page? Damn virus!

Disgusted, he turns and stares at the world outside from the window above the sink.

E – *(Loud)* What the hell?
B – *(Nervously, off stage)* What is it?

The Blue Leash

E – Come here! This guy in front of our house. What kind of bullshit -

B – Ed! Stop it! *(Pause)* Which one? So many people are walking these days. Yesterday, I had my mask on . . . you can't tell who's who -

E – There's a guy out here on the corner of Bell, and he's got a leash.

B – I'm doing a load of laundry. Do you need anything done?

E – No. *(Pause)* What is he doing?

B – *(Betty, late 70s, wearing flowered yoga pants, neon green top and shiny, black Nikes, playfully jogs into the kitchen.)* Who are you talking about?

E – *(Looks at her outfit)* Who am I married to? Jack Lalanne?

B – I'm going for my walk in a few minutes. What's wrong?

E – *(Points out the window)* That guy is what's wrong! He's walking by himself.

She moves him over so she can see out the window.

B – What's wrong with that?

E – Look! He's got a goddamn leash. A long, blue leash!

B – *(Looks out the window)* So? That's the teacher. He lives down the street with his wife. Next to the Bensons.

E – What about the leash?

B – What about the leash?

E – Why is he walking with a leash?

B – Maybe his dog got loose.

E – But he's not yelling his name or anything?

B – He has that Japanese dog. Looks like a big fox.

E – No, look! Look! He's acting like he's walking his dog!

B – *(She looks again)* That's sort of sweet. Oh! Maybe his dog died! That's so sad.

E - But why walk around the neighborhood with a leash without a dog?

B – He probably misses him.

E - So?

B – Maybe that's why he has the leash.

E – But he's acting like he's walking the dog.

B – *(As she walks away)* That's probably what he's doing. *(She takes fruit out from the refrigerator)* You want any breakfast?

E – Who does that?

B – Someone who loves their dog.

E – Stupid ass. Probably thinks the dog's in heaven, too.

B – Maybe he is in heaven. Or at the Rainbow Bridge.

E – What bullshit is that? A rainbow bridge?

B – Watch your mouth! When a pet dies, they go to the Rainbow Bridge and wait for their owners. Then when the owner dies, they cross the bridge together into heaven.

E – Is that before or after the unicorns?

B – *(Starts making a protein shake)* Why does it bother you so much? He's just –

E – *(Shouts)* Oh my God! He's stopping at the tree! Like the dog is peeing or something.

B – *(Laughs)* That's cute! Maybe you'll do that when I die?

The Blue Leash

E – Maybe you want to go walk with him, too?

B – Ed, just stop! Get away from the window.

E – What's next? Is he going to pick up imaginary poop?

B – Ed! Go read your paper.

E - These people drive me nuts!

B – What people?

E – People that pretend they're victims. If you want to mourn, go in your house and mourn. That's what the Bible says. Shut the door and mourn. Or go visit funeral homes!

B – I thought you liked dogs. You like Mookie, your brother's dog?

E – Yeah, sure, I pet him a bit, but I won't go nuts when he dies.

B - For some people dogs are like people.

E – But they're not.

B – *(Starts the blender)* Not what?

E – PEOPLE! *(Blender stops)* Dogs are not people! People are people.

B – Maybe we should get one and find out. You know I always wanted one?

E – He's probably a stupid liberal.

B – Too early for that, Mr. Hannity!

E – You think the Beef would walk around with a leash? Or Rusty? Or Tim? You think these guys would give a shit if their dog died? You say thank you, you were great, good . . . good-bye. You say good-bye, and you get another one.

B – *(Starts stretching)* So, when you die, I should just say good-bye and get another husband?

E – I said they're not people. They're dogs! In some countries, they eat dogs.

B – But for most people in the United States, they're like family.

E – Not really.

B – They are! My sister treats Marciano like he's part of her family. He sits at the dinner table. He gets haircuts, goes to daycare. She takes him shopping, vacations, everywhere!

E – Hello? That's your sister.

B - He's been to Paris! I'VE never been to Paris.

E – That doesn't make him family.

B – No, loving them makes them family. Something you seem to be lacking these days.

E – Now you're being an ass.

B – No, you are! All you see is something that needs to be fed and walked. I don't think you could love a dog.

E – Wrong! But they're not people! Can they work for a living? Can they pay the rent? Can they drive a car? Can they cook their own dinner?

B – Your mother doesn't cook her own dinner anymore! She doesn't pay her rent or drive her car. Is she an animal?

E – Watch it!

B – Her caregiver walks her every day. Maybe she's a dog?

The Blue Leash

E – You are such an ass.

B - Dogs breathe, eat, walk, cry, and laugh just like humans. They show compassion, love, sadness, joy. They're more well-rounded than most of your friends.

E – Fine! But walking around the neighborhood with a leash? That is fucking insane!

B – *(Stops stretching)* You watch your mouth!

E – Sorry.

B - *(Pause)* Why do you wear that stupid cap?

E – What?

B – Why do you wear your cap every day?

E – Because it's who I am! USS Arizona BB-39!

B – No, that was your dad's.

E – Exactly! I am my father's son. December 7, 1941! *(Coughs a few seconds)* Don't ever forget!

B – Very brave man. Wonderful husband, father.

E – Damn straight.

B – You go to the cemetery. Bring flowers. Pray at church.

E – That's right. He's why I went to Vietnam. Not like your family.

B – I know. So proud of you. *(Pause)* So, why do you wear his cap?

E – Because I'm proud of him, and I miss him every single, rotten day.

(Ed pulls out a medal from his pocket, settles into his chair, and holds it tight.)

B – That's why you wear it when we go for our walks. Or when we go shopping or to restaurants or the movies.

E – Damn straight.

B – Damn straight. Some people would say you need to get over it.

E – If those cupcakes are offended, fudge em!

B – That maybe you're just looking for attention.

E – Well, I'm not. Let them get over it. This cap means country. Loyalty. Honor.

B - I know. And the medal you take out every time you're upset? Whose is that again?

E – M. Davis. Sergeant First Class in my unit.

B – Why do you carry it around?

E – You know why.

B – I forgot.

E – *(Pause)* If it wasn't for him, I'd be dead.

B – But why carry it around? Why do you put it on your nightstand before you go to bed and pick it up before you come out here for your coffee?

E – I just do.

B – Does it bring you good luck?

E – No.

B – Do you think I'm going to steal it?

E – Maybe.

B – Do you want to keep thinking about the war? Or about him dying?

E – No.

The Blue Leash

B – Then why do it?

E – *(Pause)* I don't want to forget him. I owe him that.

B – Good. Do you think you'd forget him if you didn't have the medal?

E – No, but it helps me remember. You wear your mother's crucifix!

B – Yes, I do. *(Touches her blouse)* She got it for her first communion.

E – Because it reminds you of her, right? So, we're even.

B - I feel like she's always with me. Like she's protecting me.

E – See, you wear stuff. No harm in it.

B – None at all.

E – You wear that stupid plastic ring around your neck, too!

B – Do you remember where I got it?

E – Yes, it was in my Cracker Jacks box.

B – Our first date. Do you remember the movie we saw?

E – Uhm . . . "Son of Flubber"?

B – "The Great Escape." Steve McQueen. We sat in the back row, and you tried to kiss me before the lights even went down.

E – *(Smiles)* I don't remember doing that.

B – You do, too! *(Laughs)* And why do I wear this "stupid plastic ring"?

E – Because that's the night you fell in love with me.

B – That's right. You were smart, good looking, protective, and you had this wonderful sense of humor back then.

E – I tried.

B – That night was one of the best moments of my life.

E – *(Pause)* I don't want a dog.

B – What? I know. After forty-four years, I think I know.

E – I don't want a dog because I had a dog.

B – You did not. When did you have a dog?

E – During the war. German Shepherd.

B – Are you serious?

E – They flew thousands of military dogs in to be scouts. Our troop was assigned one. I was his handler.

B – Why didn't you ever tell me?

E – *(Silence)*

B – What was his name?

E – Major Davis. M. Davis

B – Stop it. WHAT?

E – One morning my unit was out scouting. Major signaled to me we were walking into some kind of trap. I yelled cover, my troop scattered, but the bastards shot him. *(Takes out medal.)* They gave me his medal for heroism when I got back.

B – Why did you say it belonged to somebody else?

E – I didn't! He was a Sergeant First Class.

B – But you never told me he was a dog?

E - Because he was a dog! He was more than a dog, but . . .

The Blue Leash

B – *(Stunned)* I can't believe you never told me.

E – You never told me how much that ring meant to you.

B – I've told you several times. Incredible.

E – Maybe.

B - Is that why you never wanted a dog? But you carry his medal every day?

E – I owe him. *(Looks at the medal, to himself)*. I never got a chance to say thank you. Or good-bye.

B - Holy shit! Who are you?

E – Betty, stop it. I'm your husband.

B – *(Goes over and kisses him)* You are something else.

E – And not a great one at that.

B – No, you're a damn Martian. With a beautiful heart.

E – Can we eat? I'm hungry.

B – Are you kidding me?

E – Looks like you made a protein drink for yourself.

B – I'll make your breakfast after my walk. Can you wait?

E – Maybe.

(She looks out kitchen window, and sees Scott with the leash walking back towards their house.)

B – Do you want to come?

E – Why? What would that do?

B – I don't know. Let's find out.

The Blue Leash

The Prince
(circa 12/31/2019)

Lost centurion. Empty pillow.
Rational voices rant!
Lost professor. Unspoken wisdom.
"Anthropomorphic idiot!"
Lost therapist. Fear festers. Patient dissipates.
"Misanthropic moron!"
Lost soulmate, companion, friend, comic, aerobics
instructor, spiritual salve.
"You are dead to me!"
I am dead to me.

"Still must we eat, and drink, and sleep, and wake again, - still bargain, buy, sell, ask and answer questions, - pursue, in short, a thousand shadows, though all interest in them be over; the cold mechanical habit of living remaining, after all vital interest in it has fled."

– Harriet Beecher Stowe

The Blue Leash

Journal #2
January 22nd – July 1st, 2020

January 22

Tonight, I warned all my dog-walking neighbors of the inevitable tragedy that's coming. "You know he, or she, is going to die? Ready or not, here they go! They are leaving you. Forever!" Well, in my head I told them. Never devastated like this before. If it were Max or Kate . . . can't imagine, and I know part of it is the shock of how sudden you left but - and this is the $24,000.00 question but why am I feeling your death so deeply? There's also this strange desire to hold onto the pain, as if it keeps you alive. I'm treading some seriously dark, deep water.

For the past five weeks, I've taken your blue leash with me on my daily walk since the two vases of your fur are too cumbersome to carry. Some people on this street or that park "humorously" comment about the "invisible dog." Depending on subsequent conversations, I usually hear, "You should get another dog." Why is this the first thing that comes out of people's mouth? Are dogs that expendable? Interchangeable? Did we replace Grandma so callously when she died? Not even pausing without processing? How does that philosophy work when long-term relationships break up? Should a person start dating again the following week? Look, Kuma, when you came into our lives, the skies opened, the Red Sea parted and yes, it took me quite a few months, but I finally woke up and fell in love with you. For years and years and years. Then you died. Do I immediately replace you? Doesn't that significantly diminish the meaning of your life? An unexamined life is not worth living, but what about an unexamined death? If we never take the time to examine the gravity of the moment . . . if we don't stop and consciously deal with our loss . . . no, I only have so many days left on Earth, only so many hours, and I choose to walk with you until I understand my grief. In solitude. Together.

P.S. - After five weeks, passing maybe 100-150 people on the walk, a 7-year-old boy today was the first person to ask, "Why are you walking with a dog leash? Do you miss him?" Yes, I do. Thank you.

The Blue Leash

January 24

I was thinking about a journal assignment I gave to my class last year. The entry had to start with the phrase, "The only time I truly felt infinite . . ." Taken from Stephen Chbosky's *Perks of Being a Wallflower*, the main character recalls the moment he felt infinite, his authentic self, when his new friends accepted him unconditionally, giving him a space to be himself for the first time in his life.

It reminded me of a summer long ago, maybe when you were eight or nine. OK, not that long ago. Anyway, we spent a few days up in Cambria. The weather straight from New England, the beach like the cold Atlantic shores, and the obtrusive air pinching our cheeks, but we brought our sweatshirts, windbreakers and beanies. We sat down on the beach, the kids scuttled in the damp sand while Mom and I spread out our blanket and chairs. Then, at one point, you pressed your body against mine, using me as a shield from the wind. Your head slid down on your paws as you curled into a cinnamon roll, as the dying sunlight focused on your face's noble countenance. Kate whipped out her iphone, capturing a photo series worthy of a Facebook album and while she snapped away a complete portfolio in minutes, you looked up at her and then turned to me and said, "This is great, Dad. I love being here." I'm sure you did. We both felt infinite. I'll never forget it. Actually, I'm looking at the pictures right now.

January 26

Very strange. Almost macabre. Today presented me with a walk of gratitude. WHAT? Yes, well, I'm usually weighted with sadness cause I will never see you again, or touch you, hug you, or squeeze you, but today there was a smile on my face. Life can be a string of broken dreams, of could haves and should haves. Of failed chances and misguided mistakes. Didn't make a million. Didn't become a paid actor. Didn't change the world. Didn't become a paid writer. But I married an incredible woman who gave me two beautiful children. And we created a family who loves each other every single day. And I had you. Tattooed onto my skin, flowing through my blood, permeating my gray matter. You made life bearable, enjoyable, lifting up my heart and making me laugh for more than eleven years. Best years ever. Thank God.

I remember Kuma shaking in my arms before he died. He lost his eternal calm, his James Bond demeanor, his signature sangfroid. It literally hurts me. It haunts me. I question so much about that final night. His trembling, his nervousness, his searching eyes, and his inability to understand the gravity of the moment. As I watched what was happening to him, something happened to me. The chill of helplessness labeled me as a failure and useless, stripped me of my vaulted sense of self. Later, when he had left us, or when I left him, I darkened the living room, and sat there wondering if all his vulnerabilities were not exposing me to my own. That my

The Blue Leash

self-esteem was inflated and incongruous with my true self. As if overcoming obstacles early in my life made me stronger and better than those around me. That I always felt somewhat impervious to tragedy because I never matured enough to shed my adolescent invincibility. That I never really considered my death. Everyone else's but . . .

January 28

I'm on the corner of Mountain and Chester. Whenever we turned this corner (#2 route) you would bury, I mean BURY your face in the bushes; I could not stop you. I'd count "1-2-3-4-5," my only successful way of making you move before pulling you after 5, but you didn't care; you went into some hypnotic doggie state. Maybe sensory overload. We usually met Angelina, the poodle, on this route; the closest you've ever been to having a girlfriend. I just saw her tonight. You'd follow her up the hill, chugging up the incline, losing energy along the way. You also enamored the two older ladies on the green porch. They would invariably call your name, give you gratuitous "oohs" and "ahhs," wave at you and talk about your "face of wisdom." They asked about you; I choked up, waved and moved along. Then I met the young couple with their brand new Shiba puppy. They asked about you. The woman welled up with tears as we talked about the blue leash, the joys and the aftermath. Hated talking about you in the past tense, but I felt closer to you tonight.

February 1

Kobe Bryant died last Sunday morning. As soon as I read it on my phone, while standing in the grocery line at Vons, I instantly became the town crier. Well, first I told the cashier, then the bagger and THEN I proclaimed it aloud. Then Aunt Nilda's mom died on Tuesday. Chris Taylor, my student, his dad on Wednesday. Monique, one of our religion teachers, her dad died at the end of the week. And on the walk today, I doggedly considered weighing your death against all of them. To measure my loss against all others, to consider your life equal to anybody else that has walked this planet, which confounds me to no end.

February 2

A gorgeous morning today. The black crows, the yellow-headed parrots, the red-crowned f---ing woodpecker nailing a palm outside our kitchen window. Poe-like birds with demonic tendencies cawing and screeching fake news, proclaiming how spring was upon us even though it's only February 1st. Felt like Nature beckoning me to leave my state of mourning, welcoming me to a new day, a new chapter in my life. **But there is no new day yet!** I can't choose to move on, to embrace amnesia without knowing why your life was so critical to my life, transcending all the other people who have blessed my life. Not my mother's death, not my father's, nor any of my friends' death has gutted me this deep or this long. What I do know is writing about you

The Blue Leash

keeps you here. Harbors you into my temporal lobe and fills me with memories and purpose.

Maybe it is a gorgeous morning . . .

February 3

A light turned off, a window boarded up, my life diminished without his encompassing stare, stubbornness, goofiness, companionship. At my age? I don't give a shit. I loved Kuma. It's my 64th birthday, and I'm flooded with gratitude for everything – parents, childhood, education, travel, marriage, home, children, health. 24 years of kitchens. 20 years of classrooms. Great friendships, relationships. Very few crosses to bear. Dodged at least 4 near death experiences, several car accidents and a German Lugar pointed at my head after being picked up hitchhiking by a man claiming to be en route to killing his cheating wife and her lover. He said I would read about him in the Atlanta Constitution the next day, but never found the news report. I have taken nothing for granted. I recognize the importance of every individual I have shared life with so I feel a sense of shame and guilt as I mourn the loss of Kuma. I feel abnormal. Stupid. I've been writing about him every day because I have nowhere else to express my grief. I can mourn anyone else's death with anyone else indefinitely but this carries a bit of a twist. I have stopped talking about it to everyone except Melissa.

My dear wife, and the best mom, who doesn't express her emotions nearly as much as I, lives in the same shadow.

Whenever we're alone, it's as if we have been given a green light to share our pain. As Melissa said last night, "He became part of our family. Everything we did with the kids – vacation, all the AYSO games, watch TV, eat together, sleep together – we did with him. And every time I came home, especially after the kids left, I couldn't wait to hug him. I miss him so much. And I know he was your dog, but he was my prince, and I can't believe he's gone."

I know I will take the positive aspects of his life with me. I will keep his dog license on my key chain like a lucky charm, his pictures on my phone like a guardian angel, and my solitude will be accompanied for years with his memory. This is not a rehearsal; this is life. Smile. Happy 64th birthday!

February 4

So, the dream on the 1st was supposedly a scene from my life. You and I were cruising around in my white Jetta, as the sunroof turned into a convertible (?), as we headed west on Colorado Blvd, passing Shogun Tattoo and Plate 38, hitting every green light. The windows were down as U2's *Vertigo* blasted through the dense humidity. You leaned your front paw on the door, head back, grinning, fang out. The music changed to Elton John's "Funeral for a Friend," and I looked over and quickly realized that "Kuma" was not Kuma! He was a fake you. An imposter! I detected it in the dream, and then I knew I was dreaming, and I quickly woke up.

The Blue Leash

Last night was the first REAL dream of "Kuma the Bear" since you've been gone. Took place in Connecticut, in my childhood home on Fleetwood Avenue. White, powder snow drifting down the frosted windows. I'm watching an NFL game on the couch, wearing a glum face. (The Packers must have been losing.) All of a sudden you jumped up and curled next to me, but I immediately examined your eyes to see if it was you. And it was. I didn't overreact; I let the scene unfold, whether it was live or happening in my dream. Either way, I felt grateful to touch you again; I knew you had died but felt you came back to see me again. You set your head on my lap, while I gently stroked your body. In the dream, I told my son I didn't believe God would ever bring you back to me, but I was wrong. God actually heard my prayers last night.

February 7

My trust in humans? A failed experiment. My parent's divorce. My first marriage. Divorce. Broken relationships. Broken friendships. Broken promises. Constant heartbreak. (Listening to Moody Blues . . . "Through the Eyes of a Child"). It's hard enough to negotiate our search for identity, acceptance, purpose, stability, and all of Gatsby's "promises of life." Most religions and philosophies claim all these goals are only found within, but what do we do while we are waiting for our personal enlightenment? We tend to trust others. We believe in others, making ourselves vulnerable, but often we end up lied to, backstabbed, or used. Even when you stand at the altar with your soul mate, trust becomes more important than love. You trust this person will be good to you. You trust this person is who they say they are but you never truly know. And so, we keep walking.

Dogs have no ulterior motives. Dogs are pure. They are not driven by achievement or power. They are selfless givers. They have limitations but are malleable. They have an ego but no need to hurt someone just so they can feel better about themselves. They, too, feel the pain brought on by the insecurities and evil actions of humans. Therefore, I realize that anyone lost in the labyrinth of finding eternal happiness would be blessed to have a fellow traveler to trust like Kuma. Those people might understand my unwavering dependency just as I did when I wrote this. I'm sure almost all dogs provide a heartfelt fealty, a haven of acceptance, and a door to personal happiness, but I have to say, objectively and with confidence, "Not like my Kuma!!"

February 9

"Come Back, Little Shiba!" I'm walking up Hill today, reliving our last walk. Same crisp air, like many a fall day in Connecticut. The towering trees on this street normally look down on the people passing by, throwing out snarky comments, but they were silent and bowed tonight. They seemed to recognize your absence next to me. The squirrels stood erect as I passed, almost preparing to

The Blue Leash

salute in reverence. Even the cars, in a solemn motorcade, commuted incognito.

After your initial surgery, the vet told me walking would help, and you and I agreed to shorten our walk for those first few days, but even your stubbornness had slowed to a crawl. As soon as the incline began, you pulled over. Your eyes looked down and away while your body begged to rest. I carried you home in my arms, the last few blocks, never feeling closer to you in my life. Very grateful for this time. Felt like Justin Timberlake in *No Time*, as the precious seconds dwindled somewhere between life and death. Same feeling I had a month later when I held you in the car on the way to the hospital. Enfolding you in your comfy, red blanket. Securely. Deliberately. Like holding a sick son or daughter, wishing I could take on your pain. Watching the anguish, the bewilderment in your eyes broke me. Made me less that night. I was not the superhero you always saw but a mere mortal once again.

I turned and thanked the trees tonight as they listened to me cry and reminisce. The sidewalk applauded the memory as I listlessly shuffled my way back home.

February 13

Not everyone needs a dog. Not everyone needs a husband or wife, either. Not everyone needs kids. But we need someone to see us, to know that we exist (*Hughie*, O'Neill). You saw me without any filter. I didn't have to be anyone else. I wasn't "teacher" or "dad" or "husband." Similar to Emerson's "transparent eyeball," I existed without any identity, seeing and being without any conditions. Our time became a shared prayer, a meditation on being present. Simple. It wasn't always this way. In the beginning, we were both a bit pig-headed, but you waited for me, and I learned to adore you, and with patience and understanding, we figured it out.

(10:30) Every year I ask my students, "Why do some students love my class, some hate my class and some don't care either way? Usually, it's because they've made a choice based on what others have told them, or what I look like or sound like. People have to be open, to be available, to everything life gives them. If you keep dismissing opportunities based on shallow or preconceived ideas, you might not recognize the blessings right in front of you."

Speaking of which, and I just thought of it this second, if the world is giving me your death, then shouldn't I be "open" to what to do next? I mean, I can choose to mourn you forever, stay static, or I can decide to move on today. Right? Right. But I'm waiting to move on when it feels natural, not forcing myself to let go before I'm ready. But when it does feel natural, I need to be ready to concede and let go.

February 14

A new phenomenon began about a week and a half ago. Within the first two blocks of route #3, about twenty minutes before sundown, I glanced across the street and saw the two of us walking together. Hologram? Time travel? No freaking idea, but it felt like a genuine out-of-body experience. I watched your head sniffing deeply into our neighbor's street plants while my body double was staring at your innocence, your instinctive nature, your furry persistence making me smile. You rustled around, turned your head back towards the sidewalk and the illusion dissolved. Joy sprinted through my veins. Saw us again today. Same place. Felt no pain. Don't tell anyone. This is just between you and me. Happy Valentine's!

February 16
Love. How big can it get? When my wife and I got married, we were perfectly content with love and happiness. How could we possibly have enough love to give to a child? We thought it would interfere with our "true love" never realizing how a child expands and multiplies love. And then we had our daughter. And our son. Wow, our love just kept expanding and expanding! Little did we know how each love teaches us more and feeds the other loves in our lives. Add in five cats along the way. Great! Then here comes Kuma! What? Selfless love? Never heard of it. You changed all of us, each one of us. Well, not the cats, but each one of us humans. Every family should have a Kuma. Every single person should have a Kuma. A dog you promise to "take care of for better and for worse, in sickness and in health, til

death do you part" and I'll walk him and feed him and ... your dog promises to do the same for you. Really hate the death part, though ...

February 27

How much time do I have left on Earth? A day? A month? Thirty years? Am I wasting my time right now walking with your spirit every day, a few days shy of the 11th week of your death? What if I believe you were the best dog ever? What if I had the Rolls Royce of dogs? The Jesus Christ of dogs? Isn't my intention, to honor the sacredness of life, both yours and mine, a profound, symbolic gesture? If I died walking you today, would I feel I was wasting my time? Regret that I wasn't being more productive? Maybe I could be tutoring or grading more papers? Or watching the news to be an informed citizen, or napping so I could recharge my body to live a longer life? It sounds ridiculous, though, when I write this, because there's nothing I would rather be doing than thanking God and you for our time together on earth.

March 5

Guilt accompanied me tonight. I didn't ask him to come; he ambushed me as soon as I turned off Chester, and he shadowed me all the way home. So, listen. You trusted me. You believed in me, but I'm starting to believe I let you down. I didn't pick up on the signals you were sick and

The Blue Leash

needed attention. When you hesitated sometimes to go for our walks? And then when you paused unnaturally during our most routine amblings? Just STOPPED on the sidewalk. Felt like you were just being stubborn. Until it was too late.

Max gave me this seven-cell cartoon of a dog being taken to the clinic to be euthanized. He's expressing his gratitude in his bubbled thoughts to his owner, ending with the cell, "Thanks for everything. I had a wonderful time." The first time I read it I had a visceral reaction, feeling this was a main cause of my pain and grief, because I didn't know if you had a wonderful time. Despite all the great moments we shared, I wasn't absolutely certain your experience was the same as mine, which has contributed to my guilt.

Did you choose to be in this relationship? No, you did not. Except you didn't choose anyone else in the family. Did you have a say in staying or leaving me? No, you did not. That you loved me unconditionally? Yes. That you waited for me every day and greeted me every day with love regardless? Yes, you certainly did. That you left when you did?

After 79 days, my eyes still feel sad.

Just because "caring is loving and loving is caring." ("Lazy on the River" by Joey Pecoraro)

March 10

I never knew how deep rivers flowed.
I've known rivers: wide rivers, thin rivers, wild rivers, rapid rivers.
Dark rivers. Sensual, intimidating, demanding rivers.
I've known rivers from decades past, as old as the flow of blood in my veins.
Ancient rivers from east and west, from north and south, and beyond.
Some rivers now dry as the desert, some still trickling with forever life.
But my soul, my soul, has grown deeper like the rivers,
How deep I never knew.
Until the flowing together of ours.
(Apologies to Langston Hughes)

March 14

Three months later, five minutes into my walk, I wept like it happened yesterday. The world still feels uncertain, random, setting me adrift without anchor. My unfounded sense of control and stability have slipped away in a ten-year nanosecond. How my daughter moved to UCSC. My son to NOLA. And without any foreshadowing or dramatic irony, you, the understudy, became my rock . . . until you weren't.

My tears flow from my 2nd biggest regret (we know the first!) - listening to my air pods more than listening to

The Blue Leash

you. That I wasn't in sync with the obvious present before me. Initially, my rationale was to utilize the time, to multi-task and not "lose time." Eventually, I felt I didn't want to impose myself on you and your journey. Whenever I stopped to hug or kiss you, you acted like you were annoyed. You'd pull your face away: "Dad, you're breaking my concentration." It reminded me of being immersed in a great book, only to be interrupted by a random person wanting to make conversation, oblivious to the joyful communication I was currently experiencing. I didn't want to be that guy. Until now. Should have been the alpha on that one. Now I walk duplicating your intention minus your intensity. To see and hear and smell my world, not for canine news but to appreciate what I missed when you were here, slowing down my anxiety-racing mind to be like you. Reminds me of an interview with one of my favorite actors, Al Pacino, "There is no happiness; there is only concentration." Only I find through concentration, I am starting to find happiness. One day at a time.

March 23

Not sure if heaven accepts dogs, but I trust you're in God's presence. In the movie in my head, God is playing the role of Arthur Hoggett in *Babe*, and as he looks down at you upon your December 14th arrival (you passed right by St. Peter), he assuredly speaks, "That'll do, Kuma, that'll do." What reinforces my faith in heaven and God is a YouTube video (*Cosmic Eye*) that pans back from a girl in her back yard to 10 billion light years away, and then reverses to the microscopic world of her body, showing the incalculable odds of this miracle called life on Earth. In the same way, if all that is possible, God's plan MUST include dogs, but I don't believe you're looking down on me right now. How can "heaven" be an eternity of looking down on Earth? No, I only hope you are waiting for me when I die. Maybe you can chew an endless bone, play catch with my Dad or take a nap for the next 10-30 years until a bell chimes, signaling my hoped for arrival. It's a longshot, I know, but it gives me comfort and isn't that what heaven is for?

I found this tonight. When our dear friend, Hamilton, died several years ago, his wife asked me to give a eulogy. In my tribute, I included these lines from Tennyson's "In Memorial":

My love involves the love before;
  My love is vaster passion now;
  Tho' mixed with God and Nature thou,
I seem to love thee more and more.

Far off thou art, but ever nigh;
  I have thee still, and I rejoice;
  I prosper, circled with thy voice;
I shall not lose thee tho' I die.

How apropos. Good night, Bear.

The Blue Leash

March 29

How many times can I say your name? How many walks can I take? How many pee stops do I remember before I forget? Woke up at 3 am, can't get back to sleep. One of the most unexpected blessings of this emotional rollercoaster is knowing your dear Mom understands. She feels the pain as deep as I do. We've shared memories of you over Luggage Room mushroom pizza, over drinks at Plate 38, hiking Eaton Canyon, driving by I Dig My Dog and every night when I tuck her into bed. Your obsession with catching house flies, your masterful techniques of begging for our dinner, your yodels demanding us to stop singing "Happy Birthday," which is why we kept singing it all year! Your frenzied dances, your tuxedo photo-ops, your ability to adapt to all the cats.

We are allowing endless space and time, finding each other more deeply in our loss.

April 3

Does the coronavirus finally put my illogical love for you in its "proper" place? Kobe's death didn't do it; Rosie's death didn't do it but a massive pandemic? I'm incapable of manufacturing a politically correct answer. I can't pretend, regardless of any personal backlash, why I'm relatively numb to thousands of people dying from a virus compared to you. Numb is the wrong word. Every night I watch the faces of Covid victims across the TV screen being remembered. Of course, I feel empathy and sorrow, but they are strangers. Same with Parkland. Atrocities in Africa. Selfishness? Stupidity? I DON'T KNOW!!!! Having lost the experience, the companionship, of someone who provided purpose, a harbor of trust, a source of laughter and love? The invaluable bonds actualized through our relationship compared to what? No man is an island, true, I am part of humanity, I am not alone, but then again, I am an old, loyal tiger struggling with how to change his stripes.

April 7

It was 100 days of walking in your honor on March 23rd. It is now 110 days. Kuma, let me tell you how this Coronavirus thing is making life crazy. I'm Zoom-teaching classes from my home office while Mom is taking meetings next to me. Schools are closed. Restaurants are closed. Feeling shades of cabin fever but if you were here, we'd be home together every single day. Premature retirement made just for us. I walked two times today – one for you, one for me. Lots of people are out walking their dogs right now because we are all quarantined. Only now we stare each other down from one hundred paces, like a showdown in Tombstone, anticipating who's going to back down first, off the sidewalk to the street. Also, you know how much I feed off my students and the classroom, but what I've been going through these past few days has infused me with gratitude. As the pain of your presence begins to fade, the

The Blue Leash

gratitude increases. Mornings I wake up now and stroke the bedspread where you would lay, smiling as I relive how your weight settled against my leg. We were so blessed.

April 23

My April Dream.

Kuma is laying on his side, not exactly on a bed but something quite similar. Almost like the den sofa. The lamp light sheds 40 watts above him as I kneel on the floor below him, keeping watch while he sleeps, stroking his head and back, adoring him as usual. There is no real panic or any tone other than chill. As I am stroking him, I start to rise up a bit to kiss his face and notice he has these scabs. Hard scabs on his skin, the size of nickels, with slight protrusions, like small nail heads in the center of the nickels. I noticed there are maybe 8-10 of these, but I stroke his head anyway. Kuma is breathing but not responding to my touch. He just continues to lay there. Eventually, I stroke his entire back and notice towards the rear he has a lump. I recognize it as a lymphoma lump, but it is almost a hump. It is large and unmistakable. But I keep stroking him a few more times and only then do I start to think, "Is it time to let him go?" I don't cry, but I try to decide if it's time to euthanize him. It feels like flies are going to start landing on his body very soon if I don't act quickly, but I continue to stroke him and stroke him, focusing on the light and his breathing, remaining completely indecisive.

May 23

On tonight's walk, the sun persists while clods of clay clouds offer themselves to the available imagination. Trees whisper and laugh at the oddest times. Birds shrug them off, spring boarding away to miraculously reconfigure again and again. Cats saunter by judging everyone with no qualms whatsoever. Flowers radiate beauty, if you notice them or not, for anyone who cares to take a second and ignore the minute. Even the bees and ants have rhythm, like jazz pianos and saxophones, speaking directly to the soul! While cars drive blind, while joggers and walkers are unaware the store is closing in five minutes, technology and social media abduct our soul and spiritual essence. Nature recedes like phantom images of the past. The perversion of relegating what is essential to our nature starves us all. Leaves us less than who we were meant to be. I was lucky. I had you. Thanks for instructing me to live the details, see the beauty, feel their potential. I love you and miss you. Happy 12th birthday!

June 3

It's over. After teaching English III for the past 19 years, I am done. During final exams this week, I took group photos of all five classes on my computer. Well, "group" photos being 20-25 individual faces from their computers at home. Covid 19. What an ironic way to sign off on the career that gave me direction and life. That animated me to stand on desks, play techno music and add "Meow!" and

The Blue Leash

"Woof!" to our everyday lexicon. That allowed me to see how fulfilling and life-affirming a "job" could be. After living in kitchens for so many years, I never believed there was a place where ideas could be bandied, where I could love so many people who shared their strengths and weaknesses, their loves and hates, their hopes and dreams. Now, to be so physically isolated and removed. To leave so many familiar, wonderful souls, to say goodbye with a click on a keyboard. Distance learning. Learning to be distant. Zoom, my ass!

I miss you today but even a little more than yesterday. You would have softened the blow, filled the void with your presence. We would have taken an extra walk today. Retirement will probably feel this unnatural after working non-stop for the last 50+ years, but I am smiling. Doesn't even feel too bittersweet. It's time. Like my last ½ marathon in Long Beach. There will be nothing to replace the energy of my students in the classroom, but I'm familiar with loss, right? As for missing you, the walks will continue to feed me your spirit. I'm sure I'll be talking to you even more, though I'll be bitching about your absence. Who do I become now? I am not a chef or a teacher or an active need-you-everyday-dad anymore, but once I acclimate myself to waking up with no responsibilities, except to be a great husband, I plan on writing about you. You will become my muse. In this very moment, I can feel it. Crazy, huh?

June 27

Every time I write about friendship, I end up quoting my mom's weary caution, "When you die, you'll be able to count your friends on one hand and still have a few fingers left. Your true friends." It's a sad commentary on life but grandma Lydia spoke truth. I sit here with friends within driving distance that I rarely see. I can attest to having a few high school friends on Facebook, a few teaching friends I left behind when I retired, and my wife - my very best friend of all time. Which makes you my 2nd best friend of all time! Positive, caring, accepting, supportive, unconditionally loving (selectively loving of everyone else)! You rolled with me; I rolled with you. You listened to me *usually*; I listened to you *usually*. We accepted each other's strengths, weaknesses, moods, eccentricities, and heavily-scented flatulence. As we got older, we slowed down together, snacked together and napped together. We were as intertwined as your twisted rawhide bone with bacon. Old souls in a galaxy, illuminated stars, siblings in the night sky. Harmonic alchemy.

July 1

Ozymandias sinks further into obscurity. Claire Simeone died tonight. Thought I was doing well, inching forward in my prolonged black veil syndrome, but this one hit too close to home. Since moving to San Francisco when I was twenty-one, Claire's friendship, along with Rosie's,

The Blue Leash

became one of the few cornerstones of my cobbled life. Born and raised on the East coast, full of intelligence, love, and compassion, she battled cancer for almost two years. She was strong and determined, animated and joyful with a genuine, yelping laugh. Mother, wife, nurse, sister, and daughter. Biked herself to work and back, the ten plus miles from Sausalito to San Francisco General, every day for years. Our family visited her last summer, the last time we ever boarded you, for our last dinner together. Sitting on top of her houseboat with her adoring husband, as Mt. Tamalpais observed, as the Bay calmed and settled, as the air bred quiet, we shared wine, food and homemade limoncello, reliving our young restaurant memories together. For my first chef position, I recalled hiring her as a line cook; she recalled it cooking with great friends but "we put out terrible food." For the past year and a half, I've been sustained by her beautifully composed Caring Bridge entries, always admiring her as the writer I could never become, as the person I could never become. Her resolute approach to her final days would have made Seneca proud, and I remain dry-eyed once again. Why?

WHY AM I NOT RAGING TO GOD? SHE WAS A SAINT! HOW CAN I SIT HERE NOT MOVED TO TEARS? DOESN'T SHE DESERVE FIVE YEARS OF WALKS? OR AN ELEGY BY MILTON OR SHELLEY? A POEM BY WHITMAN? HAVE I TRULY EMPTIED MY TEAR DUCTS?

1,300 Americans died yesterday from Covid! Over 120,000 Covid deaths as of today.

George Floyd, Breonna Taylor, Ahmaud Arbery were murdered this year.

Johnny Mandel, composer of "The Shadow of Your Smile" died. And on and on.

Seemingly, deaths register little more with me than scanning a familiar menu and ordering the regular, or filling my car with gas, or my biannual visit to the dentist. Have I felt so much pain that I've become inured to death? Then why did I fall apart on my walk last night when I imagined you sticking your nose in the ice plant on the corner of Mountain and Mar Vista? Physically trembling, my tears luging down my cheeks!! I know I've buried myself in your death, alone in gratitude and prayer for your spirit but after more than six months? Am I completely misanthropic, self-absorbed, or just numb?

My instinct assumes it was your presence during a critical time in my life that elevates your absence and significance. You spent so much time with me. Every day you looked directly in my eyes, looked into a soul you trusted with your own and loved me anyway. You communicated to me what you needed, when you needed it, and you gave me what I didn't know I needed when I needed it.

During my 20 years of teaching, the conversations I had among the faculty were normally limited to work-related entities such as lesson plans, online resources and always ended with, "So, what are you doing this weekend? Besides grading! LOL." My deepest connections were with my students as the class discussions offered refreshing and enlightening perspectives, as we shared personal opinions, anecdotes and experiences, as we deciphered every assigned text. By December, we would expand on Emerson's *Nature*, questioning, "Why should we grope among the dry bones of the past," and Thoreau's observations regarding how the "mass of men lead lives of quiet desperation," and every year I would recreate Munch's *The Scream* in front of my class: "That's what I keep thinking! Am I my father's clone? Am I living a desperate existence? How can I possibly make my life more authentic, more purposeful?"

Kuma, our long walks provided me the time and breath to pursue these questions further. These class conversations transposed into inner monologues that challenged my purpose and my goals. Your contemplative nature, your ability to walk undisturbed as I worked out these problems aloud, helped me explore a delicate balance between my exterior and interior lives. And every death, regardless of my frozen waterworks, and the rusted and clogged pipes of my memory, every death reminds me to live and love, to appreciate today, and to be thankful for every being that has guided me through my life. Do me a favor. Please greet Claire with your magnetic smile, charm and love. She deserves a Kuma right now. Love you, Prince.

BOOK III:
The Shadowlands

"As far as I can see, grief will never truly end. It may become softer over time, more gentle, and some days will feel sharp. But grief will last as long as love does – forever."
– Scribbles and Crumbs

The Blue Leash

The 125 Steps: A Trilogy

The Fear

A social being Kuma was not. He lived his life with solitary purpose, a bearded recluse changing the world by example; a canine Luddite searching for peace and quiet. He eschewed technology. Young children made him nervous. Tall men put him on defense. Older women and teenagers barely tolerable. Even restaurants and doggie parks too cluttered and chaotic. He liked white poodles from afar. He definitely admired older dogs, bigger dogs. Battle-tested "veterans of life" dogs. And they admired him as well. He walked like he grew up in Manhattan - resolute, skeptical, intimidating. Stylish, with a hint of danger. He was this way almost his entire life. If you ever met Kuma, you knew exactly who he was and who he wasn't.

My walks with Kuma became a constant in my life when he was about six months old. Over those eleven years, we shared more than 4,000 walks, using at least 15-20 different routes for 30-75 minutes per day. It was only during his last year, in 2019, when our routes became shorter, more certain; a decline quite familiar to most senior citizens. A routine similar to walking down to your favorite bar or breakfast nook, nodding to the other patrons as you walk in and ordering "the regular." Fewer routes, shorter distances, longer naps. Only the most necessary terrain carrying Kuma's most coveted scents. Even with the variables of weather, time, and sleep, our routine became quite predictable. Except for those last 125 steps.

For some reason, Kuma would suddenly downshift our modified excursion to a crawl, defying everything about his usual, elder statesman-like swagger. Starting from our neighbor's driveway around the corner until the first steps of our porch, his gait barely outpaced a rock. There was nothing different about this strip, though. No humongous hill to climb. No treacherous chestnut burrs to evade. All the wispy plants, California oaks, dead palm husks, assorted grasses and leftover poops from negligent dog owners were identical, but for some reason, after treading this patch of sidewalk for over a decade, those final few steps suddenly signaled more to Kuma than just an end to our daily walk.

The Blue Leash

The last 125 steps. Compared to his chesty trot up to this point, this deviation marked a significant shift. Commanding, coaxing, or cajoling him to speed up were useless. His demeanor became more akin to an art enthusiast ambling through the Norton Simon Museum. The corner mulberry bush became a Dali or Kandinsky, enigmatic and imbued with cryptic undertones, begging his analysis. Oh, and of course, 15 steps later, he had to investigate Rodin's one-week-old, sundried dog poop, and finally the shaggy Cerabus twins imprisoned behind the chain link fence, who greeted him with maniacal, non-stop smack, somehow became de Goya's etching of two dream-induced monsters, needing his prompt critique and approval.

The last 125 steps. Kuma's reluctance to walk home baffled me even more because he knew each walk ended with his favorite treats. Delicious "cookies" (doggie snacks) before dinner, seeing Mom after work, air conditioning, drinking from the patio fountain, and getting to rest his weary paws on the sofa to stretch, to lick, and to espy us from afar after he ate his kibble/roast chicken dinner before begging us for ours. His independence would reign supreme again and again. Why didn't these rewards entice him to go quicker? He's promised a heavenly reward, a happy-ever-after, and he slows down?

The last 125 steps. After observing this strange pattern for a few months, I inferred that his body wanted to go home, but his spirit sensed a fateful change, a largo tempo to Nature's cadence. His nose began relishing the burning eucalyptus even more from the neighboring chimneys. The seductive honeysuckle draped along every route more intoxicating. Kuma hungered to stay outdoors, to walk a little farther, breathe in a little deeper, even interact with a few more undesirable strangers. To feel the Santa Ana winds, witness the bluest sky, sniff the newly mowed grass because who knows? Carpe diem! Do not go gentle into that good night! Either way, going home meant it was over. Resignation, confinement, atrophy. Kuma's reticence summoned memories of my mom railing against moving to an "old folks home," screaming even harder to never employ live-in care, foreshadowing how "that will be the death of me." Kuma's hesitation evoked my dad's father. My 90-year-old Granddad refusing to give up his car keys or defying my Grandmother's wishes by dressing up at seven every morning to stand at the street corner and wave to the passing cars, sending them his good wishes and spirit. To hold on to his place in life, no matter how small or insignificant. To remain a part of this place, this magical, beautiful world, which is the only world he knew.

Once we got home, Kuma resigned himself to the inevitable. His tired body said hello to Mom, ate his cookies, scarfed his dinner and sashayed to the backyard. If he could, he probably would have read a book or worked on the daily crossword puzzle for ten minutes before falling into doggie dreamland, when his legs would begin to bicycle, and he'd sporadically start huffing and puffing, reliving another youthful fantasy. The tethers of aging, of watching other dogs chase tennis balls, of losing mobility and respect, of gathering aches from arthritis and hip dysplasia, of outliving family and friends. Kuma was unaware of life's price tag, oblivious to the gospel of a next life, but even if he knew, he was still not ready to go home.

The Main Event

Every day life ambushes our ordinary existence with metaphoric missiles, bombs, and curve balls of destruction, fully capable of dismantling our lives. Tragedies of all dimensions randomly crash into our world and devastate the humble anthills we call home. Hurricanes, earthquakes, fires, droughts, pandemics. Lost jobs, lost friends. Crippling expenses, accidents, and emotional damage. No one is immune or unchallenged and if it is not us, it is someone we know or love whose experiencing "what happens when you are busy making plans."

My family has averted most earthly disasters but realize good fortunes can be stripped away in an earthquake second, a head-on collision moment, or a medical diagnostic instant and so, especially after our two teenage birds left our nest, we relish those few days every year we come back together as a family. Thanksgiving symbolizes one of those rare occasions when we can rekindle our "blood is thicker than water" bond, nourishing us with enough warmth and laughter to sate our hearts and souls until at least Christmas. It also helps that we love food! I'm not sure if it's genetic, but for more than twenty years, we remain a shoal of piranhas. Our record for decimating a restaurant dessert stands at 45 seconds, but that's four spoons versus one tiny crème brulee! Thanksgiving has fittingly become an important day for our family to thank God for our blessings.

For me, it was a bit different. After 24 years of working in kitchens as a cook and chef, I become the chosen one. The one who aprons up around 8 am, installs himself in the kitchen with a typed-out menu and a bottle of Ballatore Gran Spumante until dinner is served at 3:30. The celebrants? A rotating guest list of parents, cousins, friends, and friends of friends, but Thanksgiving starts and ends with the "party of five" – Melissa, Kate, Max, Kuma and myself.

November 28, 2019. This year's feast offered a choice of Maple Bourbon Turkey with Wild Sage or Roasted Prime Rib with bourbon au jus, and sides of New England apple stuffing, Cajun cornbread stuffing, Old English popovers, Chambord cranberry sauce, roasted brussel sprouts with balsamic reduction, yam casserole, and creamed spinach. Oh, and here come the homemade desserts! We have Pumpkin Chiffon Pie with caramel, Chocolate Pecan Pie,

The Blue Leash

Chocolate Mousse, a medley of freshly baked cookies, and a 20-year-old, Fonseca tawny port! Of course, we ate too much once again. Everyone ended up moaning with gluttonous ecstasy until Kate, sitting on the floor and petting Kuma, asked, "Dad, have you seen this on Kuma?"

"What?"

At first, I panicked; then I stopped existing. Oxygen abandoned my cadaver. Quicker than a Monty Python foot smashing through the dining room ceiling, my brain darkened and shriveled.

"What?"

In times of survival, we have two responses. My mind chose flight, so I got up to run back into the –

"Yes, yes, I see it."

My heart forced me to touch it, absorb it, accept it. It was a lump next to his male waterworks. A hardened piece of clay, a small pumice stone unable to scrub itself away. My mind rammed into a brick wall. Weren't we supposed to be having fun? Isn't this Thanksgiving? The light in my life shattered to black. Family and friends offered me "benign this" and "previous harmless lumps" of that. Empirical examples turning into nothing blah, blah, blah . . . never were my feelings for Kuma so clear. To me.

Me *(finger-in-the-dike response)*: "Uhm, well, he doesn't look like he's in pain. When I press it, he doesn't grimace or moan. I'll bring him to the vet tomorrow. Let's play Trivial Pursuit." Very dad-like. Calm, logical, don't panic or overreact. Don't show how devastated you are even though everyone here, except me, knows how Kuma is my rock.

November 29, 2019. The next day. Vet *(compassionately stoic)*: "We took a sample. It's a fatty tumor. Benign. You can leave it alone, but it will eventually start irritating him when he pees." Whew! Dodged THAT bullet. Anxiety gone. Champagne literally popped.

December 1, 2019. Two days later. Removed. Easy peasy! I picked him up as soon as possible. Vet *(confidently)*: "He's as good as new." Poor guy's wearing the cone of shame. Funny, but dismal. He hates cones. Bought him a few new toys, some fresh chicken breast for dinner, but the medication did its job as the family hugged and kissed him to sleep. We were all happy and grateful to be home together again.

December 4, 2019. Three days later. A putrid smell noticeably emanates from Kuma's crotch while he's lying in his bed after lunch. Once again, Kate investigates and over her iphone speaker, her boyfriend diagnoses how the rancid smell "quite often means there is an infection." Thirty minutes later, we're in the emergency hospital. Yep! The stitches became infected. Major cleansing, more antibiotics, and home once again. Dodged THAT bullet.

The Blue Leash

December 6, 2019. Two days later. Follow-up at the vet. "The infection is gone. Everything looks great, but . . . *(you could fit an ocean liner after that "but")* I feel a slight bump next to his stitches. It doesn't feel right. I'd like to take a sample to see that it's nothing to worry about."

December 7, 2019. Next day. Follow-up at the vet. X-rays are placed on the film viewer. "Kuma has multicentric lymphoma. His chest, his back and his right haunch all have lumps." Direct hit. Call out the National Guard. Immortality was not an option.

December 8-12, 2019. Can't get appointments. Everyone I call – the referred oncologists, the veterinarians, the technicians – all acting like this is routine, like there's no rush, a few extra days won't hurt. Like cancer will pull over to a rest area and promise "to stop being so aggressive." *Thanks, Mr. Cancer!* Five long days of waiting. Consuming every non-sleep moment with Kuma - photoshoots and selfies, naps, dinners, philosophical discussions about time and God.

December 13, 2019. The next day. 3 p.m. Referred oncologist: "I reviewed all the tests from your vet. We have two choices. Radiation three times a week for three to four weeks, which at Kuma's age would be hard. He would not be happy coming here that many times. It might extend his life six to nine months, but during his treatments, it would not give him the quality of life we always talk about. Second choice? Prednisone. Steroids. You can give it to him at home once a day. It will extend his life one to three more months, and he'll even gain back some healthy, positive days along the way."

"Third choice? Kidding. Let's go with steroids."

I'm thinking, "We can do this. 1-3 more months. The kids come home in a few days for Christmas; our 12th year of celebrating New Year's in Santa Barbara together. One final, poignant moment we can all savor together. After that, I'll treat each day of 2020 as a blessing, a divine gift to be his nurse, his caregiver, his hospice person." How quickly I clung to the final verdict, but Kuma already knew this visit did not go well; he just wanted to go home. Before we left, he got his first daily dose of steroids, parting gifts of healthy food and natural snacks, and a reprieve from the governor!

On the way home, Kuma and I talked about what the next few months would be like. I showered him with my unending love and acknowledged our dream of retiring together in five months may be unrealized, but I vowed to share "every minute of every day that I can! Just three more days of exams before Christmas break, and I will adore you for the prince that you are. Like the prince you've always been to me." Kuma's countenance did not change. His eyes stared straight ahead at the traffic. A few

The Blue Leash

times he turned his head, his face reminding me, "Really. I just want to go home." And that's what we did.

Neither of us expected how fast the steroids would rejuvenate his body. Within hours, he began wrestling his rawhide bone, acting like his zany Shiba self, and at one point, in his infamous prone position, he stopped and stared into the multiverse. Months of ennui and his post-surgery debilitation instantly shed like a cocoon. Even he was amazed! He graciously danced, hopped, and darted around the living room, tapping his overgrown nails, flashing his toothy grin. But what lit up the living room, what was missing and now found, was the twinkle in his eyes. A twinkle expressing happiness and gratitude. Then, after about an hour, a la Cinderella's coach, he turned back into a pumpkin.

December 14, 2019. The next day. Kuma died.

*[Play "The Long Road" by Eddie Vedder
for at least 57 seconds and then . . .]*

At 1:30 in the afternoon, our last walk together was our last walk together without knowing it was our last walk together. Shrouded in a drizzly, uncertain sky, we slowly circled the lifeless park. Kuma's aging, white face, framed in his fiery red fur, woke up the miserable landscape, but his curious sniffs were less curious; his dagger stares more like wobbly camera shots. His head never rose above a whisper until I bent down to kiss his face. He asked me to cut the walk short, so we did a 180 back home. Kuma retreated to his bed, nudging and clutching his Lakers blanket like a sick child, searching for a familiar warmth.

About an hour passed before Kuma's physical cues divulged his tenuous future. My skeptical mind denied their import. Refused their implications. When he rejected his favorite beef jerky. Watching his lethargic steps to his food bowl. The disoriented stare at his favorite kibbles. When he laid on his side as his back legs twitched and trembled. Several haunting, high-pitched yodels. Increased, labored breath. His face diminishing, his dilated eyes searching for an escape, or an answer, guiding him to the corner of my darkened office, a place he'd never been, before returning to his bed two minutes later. His breathing decreased. His exhales rose in prominence. His last conscious act, a final stumble onto the sofa to lay next to me. To be with me. To comfort me. To prod me. Our lives were unraveling, a few fragile hours condensed into a few unforgiving, indestructible minutes.

A lifetime of 24/7s ending in a night of wreckage. A disease ambushing Kuma and my unwavering love. His immortality taken. The twinkle in his eyes displaced by confusion and helplessness. Thunder storms never incited such fright and panic in my boy wonder. With all his strength and self-assurance stripped, all he could think of doing, his one final, conscious act, was to lay next to me.

The Blue Leash

"His count of enchanted objects had diminished by one."
– *The Great Gatsby*, F. Scott Fitzgerald

Those last few hours, googling your symptoms, ignoring the tally, adamantly holding onto our "normal," before telling Mom we can't wait anymore, tore through my heart. We had to let you go. Lifting you in my Clark Kent arms, gathering you reassuringly, securely to my chest for what I foresaw as our last night together on Earth. Calming my voice, holding my tears, commanding my body to brace your body without flinching, giving you all my strength, capturing every ounce of you in sight, in smell, in touch . . . you were trembling, shrinking, more vulnerable than I've ever seen anyone in my life. I asked your Mom to take our picture right before we closed the door; she took two. I kissed you so hard as we were leaving, tattooing my love all over your soul, neither of us wanting to accept our fate, but propelled by circumstance to play it out.

As Mom drove us to the emergency hospital, I stared at you wondering how could you be so sick? You were beautiful! You glowed with all your majestic colors, topped with that perfect, black licorice nose. Your glorious eyes revealed a divinity most of us pray for our whole lives. My hands burrowed deeply into your bristles of magnificent fur. Your harmless paws nervously tapped my knee. And I know, I know you did everything you could to tell me it was time, but I refused to accept it. Your mortality revealed itself to me, and I was not ready. I was not ready.

But, as improbable as life itself, in spite of my selfish desires, and initial failure to recognize you were dying, the choice was easy. I struggled with bringing you to the hospital, but you were in terrible pain. Tomorrow promised only more pain. The choice was easy. I struggled because I'd never been in a position to take a life, and I didn't want yours to be the first. I didn't want to accept you had to go. I didn't want to accept it was my fatherly duty to let you go. As quickly and as painlessly as possible. I didn't want to live without you, but when I held you in the car, when your eyes whispered to mine, the choice was easy.

The Aftermath

Listening tonight to Bob Dylan's epic lament, "Murder Most Foul," an unraveling of memorable figures and fragments from America's sordid past, centered around the assassination of President Kennedy. Dylan's gravelly voice drips the weight of cynical despair, of historic exhaustion, as the ballad details the orchestrated murder of JFK and the country's last shred of "innocence," paralleling a political darkness still rippling through America today. At the same time, he invokes a litany of 20th century artistic milestones, recalling the musical balm needed to soothe our national sorrow and spiritual pain. A list of iconic singers and songs offered to ease our spirits and

The Blue Leash

help our sanity as we mourned our greatest loss. But it was too late – his death changed us forever.

On November 22, 1963, I stood on my chair in third grade, looking out the class windows, completely confused why our school buses were lining up in the driveway. Sister Andrew's pained and sober announcement over the loudspeaker instructed us to leave quietly when our bus number was called. Death permeated St. Mary's School. When I got home, my mom and dad were crying, staring blankly at the TV, frightened, a tableau of every American household. They hugged me like there was no tomorrow. It felt like there might not be. The only time in my life when the world stopped for death, possibly the last time it ever will.

The death of a president resounds across a nation, as expected, but anyone's death can equally affect multitudes. How many people knew the victims of 9/11, but how many more were profoundly changed? How many didn't know the Sandy Hook schoolchildren but were still lessened by their death? To what extent each death reverberates remains immeasurable and unknown, but the potential for its residual consequences resides in each one of us.

Four hundred years ago, John Donne's meditation on death set the bar for humanity:

"Any man's death diminishes me, because I am involved in mankind; and therefore never send to know for whom the bell tolls; it tolls for thee."

Scott D. DoVale

But can we possibly live this way? Every day our sensibilities dodge a media-driven barrage of images exploiting death. We avoid the uncomfortable talks, the references about dying because they infringe upon our daily lives. Because if we truly felt diminished by every person's death, we would be immobilized or stop existing within a week. Every ambulance and police siren we hear. Every street light with votive candles we see. Every Columbine and Parkland. Every murder, every suicide. Every 9/11. Every Covid death. Reminding us again and again of our own humanity, and with every death, we become afraid of losing another sliver of our innocence, of our joy, of believing in the finite magic of life.

But the paradox is death teaches us how to live. A process learned by having an indirect experience. The loss of a distant grandparent or a close relative. A tragic accident of a friend. The fateful loss of a parent, brother or sister. A family pet. Even while counseling on the Los Angeles Suicide Hotline for several years, after having innumerable conversations with people seriously thinking about killing themselves, I had to reassure my family and friends these were not depressing conversations but rather life-affirming talks. Conversations evaluating life and death, unraveling the figures and fragments of someone's past. Talks I never had with anyone in my personal life were beginning to help me face my fears about my own mortality.

The Blue Leash

Kuma's last 125 steps. The reluctance to get to the end. Like after your best vacation, when you lay in bed reviewing where you went and what you did, cherishing it one more time before you return back to your normal life on Monday morning. Or when you watch your son or daughter walk across the graduation stage. Maybe while you're attending a wedding or a funeral when you stop, pull back and take it all in. Those moments in our lives that give us pause, allow us an interlude to examine our existence, to review the culmination of a life with a new set of eyes and a deeper understanding. To appreciate our next few steps before they disappear as well.

Play *Evermore* by Swift
And *Aurora* by Hans, don't ever forget
Play *1-800-273-8255* by Logic and *Yui* by Ampyx
Play *Everybody Dies,* it's so sad Billie knows.

Each piece of our finite self, our hope in mankind, even our divine purpose, can be eroded over a lifetime, a time insisting we carry on. That we rush to work. That we move up the ladder. That we fill up our social calendars. That we earn a million likes. But I get it now.

   Slow down. Stay present. Read a few more books, enjoy the natural world, take a walk, say a prayer, hug family and friends, serve others. Slow it all down. Meditate. Stop drinking coffee. Stop multi-tasking! Stop speeding on the freeway. Pull over. Take the blue leash and walk. Smell the burning eucalyptus. Watch the sun hide behind the houses. Breathe. A death most foul. Listen to my musical balm. Breathe. Walk the 125 steps. And breathe.

> Play *What a Wonderful World* by Louis Armstrong
> Play *To Be Happy* by Joey Pecoraro

The year before my father died, he visited me in Los Angeles and on our last day together, before bringing him to LAX, we stood on the Pacific shore and gazed at the blue horizon. Hymns to the silence. To the beauty. To being present. Failing to hold back his tears, he tightened his arm around my waist, and said, "I'm really going to miss this place." I knew what he meant. This life. This Earth. This place of love and hate. This place of light and dark. From east to west. From dawn to dusk. From the youthful joys of invincibility to the fragility of old age. From the days of awe and wonder to the rippling effects of Kuma's death.

> *"What a hard act to follow, second to none."*
> **– Bob Dylan**

The Blue Leash

10 Things I Regret

1. Getting mad at you. In general.
2. Listening to my earbuds during our walks.
3. Getting mad when you ate the cat food
4. Getting upset when you were sniffing too long on our walks!
5. Not creating an Instagram account for you (although I have no patience for this)
6. Not recognizing your cancer earlier
7.
8.
9.
10.

"And the memories of all we have loved stay and come back to us in the evening of our life. They are not dead but sleep, and it is well to gather a treasure of them."
– Vincent van Gogh

The Blue Leash

The Presence of Absence

Submerged in my cushiony blue sofa, my head resting on two owl-themed pillows, with an ancient novel pitched on my stomach, I close my eyes, breathe deep the sandalwood incense, and smile. A smile steeped in tranquility. Completing my stay in nirvana, my right arm surrenders to serenity and reaches down to stroke my beautiful Kuma who is no longer there. My smile shrivels and disappears.

    More than six months have passed. Still adapting to life minus Kuma. Waking to a lonely bedspread, two empty bowls, and a deserted backyard, I routinely stir my coffee and walk over to his urn, adorned with Leibovitz-worthy photos, a tall Scooby-Doo candle and the engraved "KUMA: 2008-2019" tomb marker. Cry. Smile. Laugh. Talk to him out loud. Miss his doggie breath on my pillowed face. No more stuffed squirrels dropped at my feet. Not even an apparition staring at me from across the street anymore. Quite often, I end my nights impersonating Heathcliff's demand to Cathy's spirit: "Be with me always, take any form, drive me mad. Only do not leave me in this abyss, where I cannot find you!" Melodramatic but honest, as the void increases with the silence, while the silence amplifies the loss.

Life itself lacks Kuma's presence. His body refocused rooms. His spirit electrified friends and strangers. His style embodied sangfroid, and his infamous stare was the Hemingway of canine communicado. If he lacked anything, he'd lift his head and look me straight in the eye. And I would know. At dinner, he'd sit next to my right leg, avoid my eyes and stare at my food. A stare not quite yearning or requesting or demanding but exhibiting gravity. The food was no longer mine. Now, his absence sits like the proverbial, non-existent elephant in our rooms and in my life.

As the universe would have it, around mid-June, weeks after my retirement, my Heathcliff-ian request had been answered. Without tapping my ruby slippers three times, or signing a Dr. Faustus contract, Kuma's presence revealed itself to me, residing in plain sight, in every room in our house. Under my desk, next to the fireplace, on my bed, below the bathroom heater, across the sofa. Priceless tufts of Kuma's illustrious fur and his charming alpha spirit

The Blue Leash

left behind on my passenger seat for my sanity. How he requested kibbles here, threw up Bermuda grass over there. How he parked himself in the kitchen during dinner prep. How he leapt around on our bed in pursuit of flies. What I was subconsciously avoiding for months became my deliverance - my 40-pound specter still lived!

Whenever I've lost someone in my life, an integral part of my makeshift life support includes a stream of memories and a stretch of magical thinking. Thoughts of their gentle touch, inimitable voice, brazen language, or infectious laugh help me recall each person's significance and soften the loss of their presence. But my memories of Kuma, recent and voluminous, evoke even more - a deeper, almost forgotten form of my past self. As in Wordsworth's *Lines Written a Few Miles Above Tintern Abbey*, his return to a familiar part of Nature reacquaints him with who he was and who he is as "the memory recalls and refreshes in the etched past," so, too, do the vestiges of Kuma. Critical moments imbued in my home, not to encourage me to dwell on the loss but to relive our time together, which rekindles my own joy and spirit. Kuma feels like he will always be as accessible and fruitful as Tintern Abbey. But for how long?

When my daughter and son moved out for college, their bedrooms were left untouched, assuming the status of sacrosanct museums exhibiting their childhood relics and artifacts. My wife and I knew neither of them were returning, but we never discussed evicting their spirits or personal paraphernalia. Of course, each room could be reimagined as a guest room, storage room, or office space. Yes, I'm sure we thought about taking down the Coldplay posters, selling the captain's bed, and redoing the hardwood floors, but why? Their current state offered so much more to our lives, a gateway to a warmer time, a deeper, more purposeful version of ourselves. They lessened our loss, eased us into letting go, and allowed us a chance to mourn our children's absence. Looking at school play programs, penciled stages of growth, cheerleading shoes, sheet music, dried roses, athletic trophies, black-framed graduation pictures. What a blessing to smell their scent, to relive our talks, hugs, and loving "Good Nights!"

In the same way, Kuma's effects remain untouched, allowing me to relive my time with him again. Not just imagining his angelic face looking down from the heavens, but his empirical presence awakening the best of myself and allowing me to see life through a wider lens. He disrupts my staid existence by evoking his spontaneity. He tacitly requests me to restructure my life, and to write about his, while I paste my office walls with his image. He reminds me not to take myself so seriously and to live in the present by mindfully incorporating the past. Any pain of seeing Kuma's stuffed toys or personal effects dissipates when compared to the happiness of reliving our companionship.

Right now, Kuma's bed dominates the living room like a town's celebrated monument. We bought it only because

The Blue Leash

we got rid of Kuma's sofa without immediately replacing it. So, to diminish his disappointment, I bought it. From the first time he laid down, he looked like Al Unser sitting in a custom designed Corvette; it became his second home. Everything in the room revolves around it, like the Arc de Triomphe, as it redefines our living room and our lives. The Z Gallery floor lamp recedes and the heirloom chairs retreat. Our guests are now handed brochures upon entrance, to appreciate the bed's historical and familial significance, before resuming the customary home tour. His bed commands attention and enduring, bittersweet memories.

His red, Schroeder blanket, draped over his bed, embodies the 2-year-old Kuma, who decided he needed it more than my daughter. It was his first time away from home. We were going to lunch in Ventura, didn't quite know what to do with him at the restaurant, so we brought the blanket and placed it on the sidewalk. Without a word, he laid on it and played security guard, his countenance unusually alert and defensive, occasionally looking up to me for his next command. Ears peaked. Ready. There were also times when I bogarted that blanket on the beach, but he'd push me off like a homeowner evicting a trespassing squatter. Another time an unsupervised, wandering boy wandered too close to the blanket so Kuma nipped him on the ankle. No blood, no foul.

Kuma's crate, emblematic of his entire persona, remains a fixture in our bedroom. Large, demanding attention, adaptable to change and a satisfying place of refuge. From the day we brought him home, his crate was his castle, his fortress away from home. He slept on our bed 98% of the time, but the crate was his bulwark from earthquakes, thunder storms and unwanted cat interplay. Still untouched like our other children's bedrooms. A few books on top, a pillow or two for decorations but a priceless fixture of Rodinian proportions.

Our bed never truly "belonged" to Kuma, but he implanted his life and his spirit on it over the past decade. It's not something we would throw away after his death, but it symbolizes his softer side, the earned trust, the playful joy he exuded every night and morn. Kuma and I retreated to the bed every day I came home from teaching, either to wrestle, hug, or briefly share a late afternoon nap. Far removed from career, anxiety, decisions, technology. From walks, bones, gardeners, and endless itches. Our heads tilted into one another's on the pillow. My belly protruding from my untucked shirt; his fang protruding like a pale candy corn from his lips. My eyes closed, listening to his heart on my leg. His eyes closed, brushing his waves of tufted fur under my jaw. So easy to conjure any morning I choose. And the nights were even better as my legs and body accommodated Kuma's every twitch. As long as he was comfortable.

Ironically, the places that signify Kuma's absence grant me what the world does not – a place to mourn. Normally,

The Blue Leash

friends and family share your grief and reach out to heal your pain and loss. A few of them help you to recover your reason to wake up tomorrow but for a dog's death? There is no mourning a dog's death in a human world. At least, not beyond the two weeks one is "allowed" for losing a family pet, and the sheer volume and weight of judgement eroding most discussions. People questioned my sanity, vilified my feelings, diagnosed my childhood, and shared their disappointment quite openly by opining, "Just when you think you know somebody." Obviously, there are other dog people who completely understand, but a culture who deems itself superior to Nature and dismisses the significance of any animal's life, regardless of context, well, it does not lead to a conducive atmosphere to mourn their loss.

For months I portrayed the author/minister C. S. Lewis in the movie *Shadowlands*. Severely shaken by his wife's terminal cancer, Lewis rejected a friend's trite justification how God has a plan, exclaiming, "NO! This is a bloody awful mess and that's all there is to it." The reality of losing someone inflicts a sadness impossible to wash away with "thoughts and prayers," or "just get another dog." We all live among the shadows, walking among those souls who etched themselves into our lives. People who elevated us, nurtured us and saw us better than we saw ourselves. Kuma's presence not only continues to encourage my well-being but roars salvation to me, edifying me daily and exposing my shameful neglect of empathy for other's pain. Whitman's epiphanous line, how "every atom belonging to me as good belongs to you," finally rings true to me; doubting Thomas now touches the wounds every day and lives humbled and grateful for the honor.

    Whether it's the blue leash and the black harness, the neon Nerf footballs, the crate, the bed or the empty food bowls, whatever room they are sitting in, the presence of Kuma's absence ironically brings me peace. I take impromptu walks, write more platitudes, embrace the physical evidence of his life and talk to him every day, believing that, well, just like anyone else who dies, maybe he can see me or hear me. If there is such a place, I believe he's there, and I hope to walk with him again. But until then . . .

"Mostly it is loss which teaches us about the worth of things."
– Arthur Schopenhauer

The Blue Leash

Journal #3
July 7th – December 14th, 2020

July 7

I am not comparing the life and death of a dog to a human, but the emotional value and loss of one companion to another. It is not a sad commentary on the alienation of our culture, projecting our love and attention on something "other" than a human, nor is it great insight into the nature of the interdependence between nature and man, where balance is achieved in the apparent openness of individuals to accept dogs, cats, and those down the evolutionary chain. The question I pose in this comparison is how deep can we allow ourselves to love our furry companions before there is an unhealthy or unnatural imbalance?

Scott D. DoVale

The first time I encountered this conundrum of possibly loving a dog too much was at a birthday party. For a dog. As soon as I received the invitation in the mail (Evite wasn't launched until 1998), with a black-and-white photograph of two poodles dressed in formal wear and standing on their hindlegs, I scoffed, shook my head and RSVPed. What made this occasion appealing enough to attend was the dog's parents were also the parents of my almost fiancée – Justyne. And so, on this particular Sunday afternoon, on a hallowed strip of Wilshire Blvd, known as the "Miracle Mile," and neighboring the famous Wiltern Theater, the celebration was staged for the Duchess, a five-year-old Yorkshire Terrier.

Walking into the semi-formal, catered affair unsettled me for a few minutes. Much like attending an intimate affair in Beverly Hills or Malibu, there were the stylish guests floating and posing around the modern art living room, toting fluted champagne, circular canapes and amorphous personas. The Stefon glass, dining room table teeming with gifts and cards. The 12-inch, white-frosted Susie Cakes pedestaled atop the baby grand, and the Duchess prancing through the room greeting her guests in her pink tutu and gold tiara. My eyes did several 360s. Even for Los Angeles, this scene articulated surreal better than any John Waters film. We all shared in very light conversation, eyes admiring the Duchess, while toasting heartfelt birthday wishes with our glasses raised. And believe me, this is not a criticism but a

The Blue Leash

world completely foreign to my reality. I was in my late 20s; dogs were not at the top of my list for idolatry or personal happiness. How could anyone be so reverential to a dog? I analyzed the room, looking for someone who shared my disbelief, or the situational incongruity, but I stood alone.

Years later I made the unfortunate decision to not attend my cousin's memorial for her English Springer. Another afternoon affair, complete with drinks, eulogies and a personalized brick hosted at the local SPCA. In this case, my judgement was harsher. "What is wrong with her? Why would she canonize her dog through cremation and then have her ashes interred? She's lived alone for years, divorced, a wonderful career but to create a Go-fund-me page for the brick and the service?" Maybe if you're surrounded by family and friends who feel the same about their pets, but I declined to even acknowledge the event. Since then, my sincere regret and apology for not attending and for not offering any empathy has been well-documented. My intolerance publicly shamed and dismantled.

My girlfriend's parents and my cousin understood the distinction between a human and a dog, but they also recognized their corresponding spirits of love, acceptance and companionship. To memorialize the life of a dog as you would a human, to show your gratitude and respect for someone who shared with you food and shelter, who loved you unconditionally, who edified your life and your soul, makes all the sense in the world.

July 13

My 206th day of lacking the joy you infused in my every day, so I attempted to smell the mountain bushes on the corner of C and M, to understudy your experience, making your actions more ingrained and common place to me. Put my nose down to it and inhaled! Noticed a gray Chevy Tahoe lingering a few extra seconds at the stop sign to observe my behavior. "So what? Take a picture! I'm doing this for love!" I should have barked. Also, at the corner of Mar Vista and Bell, I took a few pictures and this incredible idea besieged my brain. How about a catalogue of your favorite "pee/sniff" spots of ALL-TIME!! A coffee table book highlighting your Bungalow Heaven routes and rest areas. Add some artistic shots capturing the rustic venues, the contemporary hot spots, the bars, cafes, and upscale dining places that have been graced by your presence around Pasadena. If only we thought of this while you were alive.

July 19

I'm staring at your desktop screen face tonight, the one you visited me with months ago, and your eyes looking back continue to pardon me of all my sins - anger, pride, impatience, selfishness, stubbornness. Your healing presence giving me a sense of being loved, of being valued, of being unified with you unconditionally. Throughout my life, the world insisted on me proving my value – at school, at work, at home, with friends or family. Whether through

The Blue Leash

my wisdom of life, my kitchen proficiency, my English acuity, my physical prowess, the results never left me any better. Just relieved until the next test and yes, I know, self-worth emanates from self and nowhere else. Intellectually, I understand the concept but applying it to everyday life was hard, like telling myself I'm good enough and can you say, "Stuart Smalley"? Reality taught me something much different my whole life until there was you. You kicked ass, bit ankles, warded off doubters (and the mailman) at the front door. No other agenda but self-preservation. Loving with borders. Urbane aloofness. I need that. I miss that.

Shibas, in general, and you specifically, had a consciousness beyond any other dog - the yapping Chihuahua (cute dogs), the needy Spaniel ("They look so sad") or the intimidating Pitbull ("Try to kick my ass!"). Your confidence, your self-assuredness, being content with yourself, baffled those around you and deterring anyone with an IQ above 100.

August 11

MONUMENTAL DAY. Wrote to your breeder ten minutes ago to request another Shiba puppy. Loneliness lured me to cross the line. On one level, it felt good, a Lazarus moment, to feel that your mom and I are prepared for this emotional shift. What I'm most concerned with, though, as I've mentioned before, is it feels like an act of disloyalty, a betrayal to what you meant to me and our family. I don't need to go dogless for the rest of my life to prove my love but as with anyone's death, or divorce or breakup, do you jump right back in or do you take the time to synthesize the highs and lows, the moments you cherished, the things you learned . . . when is a reasonable, respectful amount of time to mourn before deciding to "move on"? It's different for everyone, I know, but . . . well, I made the call. The dice have been thrown.

August 26

Wednesday. Five days in Santa Barbara. Every single day I've walked neighborhoods I'm sure you would remember. I'm talking the shady, tree-lined, maze-like streets, like Mason and Ortega, crowded with cream-colored condos, with clay tile roofs and arched adobe doorways, cooling in the sifted breeze. Yes, plenty of trimmed bushes, palm trees with dead bark on the sidewalk and the occasional squirrely squirrels chasing each other. A Shiba Shangra-la!

During my walk on Friday, I met a man, a short Kevin Costner doppelganger, who crossed the street to ask me about your blue leash. He smiled, knowingly laughed a bit about my heartfelt tribute, and went on to share his love for Larry the Pug(nacious), who passed away several months ago, waxing poetic how Larry personified greatness, how Kevin "could take him anywhere – hotels, restaurants, planes, trains, automobiles – and he just went." He proceeded to unveil his private "Larry' Shrine" photos

The Blue Leash

on his iphone, complete with votive candles, stuffed animals, his raincoat, and an original Larry portrait done by a friend. However, after two weeks of grieving Larry's death, his wife surprised him with a new pug, Theo, the exact opposite of Larry – stubborn, homebody, devilish. Kevin pointed to the blue sky. "I'm sure Larry's up there right now laughing, 'So, you thought you could replace me? Ha! Serves you right!'" Said he would think of you, Kuma, and hopes we see each other again. Something about sharing loss makes me see the world with a softer smile and more empathic eyes.

August 27

Hate to admit this but as I performed my daily tribute tonight, my head was besieged by traitorous notions how these walks are becoming uninspired, monotonous, and repetitive. Never, Never, NEVER (!), did they ever feel this way before. Maybe I'm tired or stressed, or it's the summer heat or school started without me so my whole existence lacks purpose. Eerily similar to the journal entry when our neighborhood was draped in greens and grays, seesawing from life to death but this was different, relating more to my life and my final days on earth.

Granted, my walks are quicker than a few months ago. I used to stop at 8-9 pee sites along the way. Then it was 4-5. Now, it's 1-2. I've incorporated a mini-Covid workout into the walk, perverting the main intent as I strive for 10,000 steps by the end of each trek. Shit, I might as well add ankle weights and watch videos. To lose my sole purpose in 9 ½ months feels quite disappointing. What's still hanging in there is my focus on the details. Not quite up to your capacity to download a neighbor dog's recent history off the Santa Susana Monkey Flower (had to look it up). Taking in what the landscape provides, but my whole demeanor right now is askew.

The most positive aspect of my life after these eight months? I'm writing.

I'm writing about you constantly. And every time I do, every day I sit and write, I'm reliving you again and again. This week I've been writing about when we first met and how I didn't want a dog, but the kids insisted. It reminded me of when we brought you home and for some reason, I thought you weren't going to grow, like Shibas were small dogs. HA! I also started a story on the history of the Shiba, imagining your ancestry from Japan to America. You have given me a new direction and purpose. Maybe writing about you emerges as our new walk.

September 20

My dearest Kuma, are you any farther or closer to me now than you were the minute you died? Has your spirit moved on? Did you linger for a day or a week, or are you still right next to me? Are you that unknown itch on my left forearm? That knock on the front door with no caller? I picture you

The Blue Leash

laying at my feet in the office almost every day I write. When I least expect it, these questions appear and without an anchor, in my recreation of your life and death, my mind drifts and spins to a cul-de-sac, to a dusty, rural dead end.

Sat in today on the Zoom memorial service for Claire. 183 people attending, 35 of them giving heartfelt comments from the corners of the United States, South Africa, and Scotland. Someone quoted Mary Oliver's poem about Benjamin, her dog. "Benny, I say, / don't worry / I also know the way / the old life haunts the new." Of course, I quickly thought of you, especially the last night sitting with you on the sofa, staring into each other's eyes, reassuring one another of our profound gratitude for one another. There was also a man on Zoom from England, young in spirit, old in years, sharing a moment in time with Claire, ending his brief eulogy by quoting Emerson's aphorism, "A friend may well be reckoned the masterpiece of nature." All in favor?

Throughout the two-hour observance, there were continuous waves of laughter and song, tales and toasts, unanimous joys showering Claire's husband and two daughters with genuine testimonies of affection. At one point, the Bay Area sun beamed through their living room's skylight creating an occult aura over the family. All the Zoomers collectively gasped and then spontaneously prayed.

An informal mourning, without pretension or conceit, held together by life-changing memories destined to live longer than anyone there. The rituals of mourning give one hope and a needed sense of peace. Yes, they help encourage closure, but there exists in man an innate desire to pay tribute, to stand up and witness when one is called, to recognize what you value, what makes this life have meaning. Mourning reveals character.

September 24

Should read my journal more. This was from 2/2/20, the night before my birthday and it says, *"Only realization today is the same one I keep mentioning. I loved my life more when he was in it."* Months and years will go by but no other words will better articulate or capture what I've been feeling since day one. Breathing allows me to sustain and bear my loss another day, but writing etches my pain. Whether I'm sitting, eating, golfing, reading, cooking, whatever I'm doing - that same thought resurfaces again and again, but carving it into my writing, my journal and my heart enshrines it deeper. Longer. My life was better with Kuma than without. I was a better person with Kuma than without. I hope someone thinks that about me when I die. Drop mike.

September 25

Taking your face in my hands, holding you as my child. As soon as I think of this, as I recall when you were a pup, this societal censor comes into my brain admonishing me for the mortal sin of elevating your prominence in my life, and my first response is STOP APOLOGIZING FOR LOVING HIM LIKE A SON!!! It permeates every freaking thing I am writing. JUST STOP!!! And I know the problem lies within. The more people allow themselves to openly mourn their canine (and feline) losses, the quicker the stigma will be dispelled. Still thinking about Claire's communal memorial as being one solution.

> On my walk, I am propelled by you
> On my walk, I am bound to you
> On my walk, I am indebted to you
> On my walk with you.

Enchanted by your Shiba charisma. Beguiled by your wily ways!! Your foxy furriness! It eluded me in our first months together as you whined and dined, but gradually, like the first time a boy becomes conscious of a girl's perfume, the softness of her smile, the electricity in her touch. Engulfed without warning. No consent form to be signed. But there I was, as a young Nick Carraway, "I was within and without, both enchanted and repelled." You did that to me. And I am not ashamed.

September 26

Finished *Call of the Wild* today. This Jack London quote about Buck exemplifies Kuma: "[Kuma] was content to adore at a distance. He would lie by the hour, eager, alert, at [my] feet looking up into [my] face, dwelling upon it, studying it, following with keenest interest each fleeting expression, every movement or change of feature." And there ends the comparison.

Buck grew up in Santa Clara Valley, the "life of a stated aristocrat" before he slowly evolved into his more instinctual, natural self in the Alaskan wild; Kuma never left his aristocracy. Not quite spoiled or entitled but far from morphing into his ancestors in the wilds of Japan. Far from adventuring out in nature to find his true calling. His purpose did not entail running with a pack; his might have been closer to becoming a Tibetan monk. He pursued peace and solitude, but our togetherness with distance, at his tacit behest, allowed him to love, respect, protect and care for all of us.

September 27

At some point, this daily walk posed the question if I would learn anything from this commitment after one year a la Thoreau's entering the woods "to live deliberately, to front only the essential facts of life, and see if [he] could not learn what it had to teach." I had no preconceived idea what might be achieved aside from honoring Kuma's memory, but it is in the doing where my reward lies. The walk became a discipline, a meditation, where I pledged to focus on something outside of myself and am quietly

The Blue Leash

finding peace within myself. In the simple act of walking to venerate Kuma's influence, I've considered my flaws, been humbled by my blessings and finding a healthier self-esteem. A stronger me.

Today's observation: Walking down Holliston, I hear a beak loudly tapping, breaking the sounds of suburban Sunday silence. A black-headed, red-breasted finch violently flutters on a shiny red Tacoma parked in a driveway. Perched in front of the passenger's sideview mirror, maybe confused, maybe feeling threatened, he abruptly stops his barrage and stares at his image. Wary of the other. Sometimes admiring his better half, and then doubting what he sees, possibly feeling mocked at the mimic. Then he repeatedly lunges at the phantom, pecking and retreat, pecking and retreat. Viciously and endlessly. Too many times I watched before I saw myself and walked away from the past.

October 4

It's not like I'm hunting for moral adversaries or existential arguments to defend my honor or Kuma's, but I've adamantly maintained how nothing in my life has wounded me more or equaled the pain of Kuma's death. That was until today.

This morning, a black-and-white photo was posted on Facebook showing an ordinary hospital room, with a young mother in an ordinary hospital gown, lying in a medical bed attached to an IV, her Covid mask on her waist, cradling her newborn daughter with twenty emotions coexisting on her worn face, while her husband's forehead was reaching down to her, touching her forehead, staring at his baby girl, shrouded in the room's dark shadows, a Nativity tableau between hello and goodbye. They were all saying goodbye. The mother was a former student of mine. Tears burst down my cheeks as the spell was broken.

In my literature class, I would always define tragedy as a calamity, a disaster, or a fatal event. *Hamlet. The Great Gatsby. Of Mice and Men.* But which is more tragic – *King Lear* or *Romeo and Juliet*? A 95-year-old man dying of cancer or a 6-year-old boy? The death of your parents or your children? The merciless slaying of innocence, the callous, premature taking of youth, of dreams and potential randomly killed, to me reigns as the greatest of tragedies, a human's most horrific suffering on earth.

I absorbed the hospital scene with no words, no analogies, no juxtaposing my loss vs. your loss. I just felt a sharp slap across my face as I stared at an epiphany of epic emotion. I felt smaller as I apologized to the photograph.

October 7

Sun reaching through the trees, a warm breeze, faint smoke from the mountain fires still lingering. Quite a few ashes settled on roofs, cars, porches, bushes. What an incredible walk! Funny how after months and months, I recognized today how "Kuma Bear" has become my mantra. I've

The Blue Leash

never had a mantra. A phrase that centers me, makes me more mindful, meditative. Focused. Appreciative. I say it everywhere I go but especially on my walks. For months my initial response to his name was sadness and loss. Today, somehow, I felt it as a bubble of release floating to the surface, of Nature feeding me the joy of having loved Kuma, as if the universe was showing me he is part of everything I see and everything I do. What a gift!

October 8

Kuma, I don't know if I'm ready for this but as you probably know, the breeder wrote last night. Our new, black Shiba puppy's birth is due around November 10th; his arrival to our house will coincide with your one-year anniversary. Apropos? Full circle? I'm not sure yet, but this question of fealty rises once again. Loyalty has always been extremely important to me. Don't know when it first started, but I've always been loyal to everything: jobs, people, grocery stores, restaurants, gas stations, and my current doctor of 20 years, even though I still question his abilities. It came up a few years ago when I started therapy to deal with my anxiety after Kate left for college. After about six months, my therapist notified me she was starting her own practice. The fee would be increased and my insurance wouldn't cover it, so she began to recommend other therapists. OMG! I was so opposed to seeing anyone else. I paid the extra money, moved our meeting time, thinking how could I possibly change? We've already shared all this time together. It definitely became a loyalty thing. Even though our relationship was one-sided, I felt a duty to stay with her.

This feeling of betrayal looms large, as if being a dad to another pup will diminish our time together, but I've discovered over these past nine months how you're a part of who I am, a part that will never die. My daily ritual of walking with your spirit. Writing about you, talking about you, looking at pictures of you every single day. Keeping you constantly present in my life. Doing all these things have kept you alive in my heart. And, yes, I've been afraid of lessening the significance of your life by letting you go and moving on, but I think that's a fear having to do with my own life. As I'm getting older, especially in the last few years, I'm worried about my own life slipping into irrelevance, losing my purpose, my identity, of not having anyone depend on me. Of becoming dependent, a burden and eventually invisible to a world that doesn't value life . . . but you were there for me. Now, I believe it's my turn.

October 9

300 days today. And what do I do in 66 days? How do I accept what I have not quite accepted for the past 300 days? Why has this one year sprinted by faster than the rest, in sadness and solemnity. I do not look forward to that day in 66 days but in my heart, it will probably feel like today.

The Blue Leash

Covid is in the air shaking everyone's reality. Empty streets, dead leaves, parched grass, naked branches, dubious sky. All contrasting but somehow conducive for me to focus on your joyful bounce, on your power and your purpose. I smiled and laughed with Nature today. Your memory sits large on Mt. Olympus today. 300 days later.

October 13

The major similarity between teaching juniors and walking Kuma? Aside from missing them both right now, it would be the feeling of living a purposeful life. Solitude is great, retirement offers me unlimited space to live, to stretch my brain and discover new things, but I seem to thrive in shared spaces of spontaneity, trust, and love. A conscious, universal buy-in where ego is gone and people genuinely focus on examining their lives. Hmmm, maybe a place where I'm in control, too! The same as acting on stage for nine years, the twenty-four years I spent working in kitchens. A give and take and a shared common goal, whether it's being in a theater production or getting food out for the party on time. Discussing the assigned chapters of *Huckleberry Finn* or spending a collaborative hour observing dogs and Nature along the sidewalks of Pasadena. I'm learning now how to operate alone, with the memories of Kuma and teaching guiding my writing, still focused on living a purposeful life.

October 24

On this very cool, crisp and sunny morning, the Santa Anas continue to whip up the ashes off the San Gabriel mountains, the remnants of the early October fires. Didn't even write down today's walk because I am trying to focus more on the walk itself, on being you. (NOW I THINK OF IT!) Very much steeped in "Kuma dreams" today as the weather not only reflects an autumn sadness but parallels the weather when you died, and then I realize your anniversary inches closer. Less than 60 walks left before my promise to you is complete. How precious this time with and without you emanates throughout my life this year, the mystical nature of walking with you, through the past and the present simultaneously.

The sidewalk has accumulated a few pine cone pods, quite a few of these tiny spiny-tooth edged dead leaves from the oaks. OMG, as you got older, you would avoid them like the plague (or as we call it now, Covid-19). Our walk would shift down into 1st gear as you navigated your delicate paws through the pedi-mine field, and then shift back to 2nd or 3rd until the next obstacle. More than a few times you pulled over to the side on somebody's lawn and refused to walk another step. Until the last few years, I never thought a spiny leaf would impale itself on your paw pads. So happy to be there, though, to reenact "Androcles and the Lion" with you.

The Blue Leash

November 1

Sunday down Mountain Ave. It's impossible to conjure up your spirit these days. My conjuring battery has died, and I misplaced its charger. Meanwhile, this teeny-weeny, gray lizard, very much like a gecko, frenetically crossed my path on the sidewalk, and you weren't there to see it. He would have startled you, but . . . and then two blocks later, those menacing pine cone babies were once again strewn across the cracked sidewalk, and I keep coming back to the fact that you are gone. You are NEVER coming back to me, and I am still here living this life. I am crying because F--K I miss you so much, and I feel CRAZY. Insane. Like I'm living a double life since mourning your death does not appear on anyone else's radar, at least no one in my life, except your mom who continues to listen to me every single day.

I'm rewriting the intro to your book now, recalling all these people who have died in my life and it's the God's honest truth - I've never cried this much. Your memory acts as an emotional tuning fork. Whenever it's tapped, it instantly vibrates inside me with resounding tears, laughter, and a familiar, lukewarm resignation.

Did I mention Thanksgiving is encroaching on the calendar? I'm sure to bury myself in the details of last year, relive every step of your passing, wishing to feel the brunt of it all once again. Take a long walk, drink a few beers and lock myself away in the office to revisit and write about my fortuitous friendship. I'm staying more present, living my more mindfully, but writing about you and walking with your leash every single day, feasting on your photos and videos every single day? Living in the shadows. Why you? "I can't escape the way I love you. I don't want to." (billie eilish - listening right now). Yes, that's it.

November 6

Went to breakfast this morning with K, a former student, who recently sought me out for some guidance. She's been volunteering at a Los Angeles suicide hotline, something I had done for many years, and she wanted to share her recent experiences regarding her counseling calls to get my perspective on her approach. Suicide prevention calls are not conversational fare; you can't talk about them with just anyone. The dialogue often digs deeper, becoming more emotional and transformative than those in our daily lives. You listen to the intimate details of strangers who are willing to share their life stories with a quickly arranged trust - teenagers on meth, cancer patients, a drunk spouse, an abused 13-year-old, a forgotten grandmother, people on the razor's edge - exposing their deepest heartaches, their personal failures, their darkest demons. Together you question life's meaning, its difficulties and blessings, its obstacles and possible solutions. Both parties share in reassessing their own values and purpose and by the end of each shift, after listening to the collective symptoms of a

The Blue Leash

city seeking an emotional refuge, the counselor walks away more grateful and inspired to live.

K and I agreed that active listening and empathy were key to understanding and assessing each caller. This technique not only helps when you're talking to those at a critical juncture in their lives, but with family and friends as well. As a counselor, you realize your safely constructed bubble does not grant you immunity to life's unforeseen tragedies. Quite often, when my hotline calls would end with the caller saying, "Thank you for being there for me," I would reply, "No, thank you. Maybe in a few years I'll be calling you." My critique of K's approach was positive. "If people would take the time, like you do with your callers, to truly listen and be more empathetic in their own relationships, it would help them heal their friends and acquaintances and help them connect to their own true nature, creating a new, healthier world to live in. And this goes for their dogs as well!"

Right before we left, we assigned each other literary "homework" to discuss at our next breakfast. I suggested "The Shortness of Life" by Seneca; K countered with Ecclesiastes. Walking to the parking lot, she asked me for a brief update about the "Kuma" book. I mentioned this past year of walking and writing was more therapeutic than I anticipated, but by honoring Kuma's spirit, I was beginning to discover why his death had affected me so dramatically.

"And what did you come up with?"

"I think I lost my hotline."

November 10

Welcomed drizzle and cold arrived during the night. Your favorite weather is here for the 2nd day in a row. I wore 2 shirts and a sweatshirt as I embarked on our great walk to celebrate our new president. Later on, newscasts showed cheering crowds in Philly, Atlanta and New York all sharing a communal sigh of relief. At least 50% of the population understood how close we were to losing our democracy. What we somehow took for granted lives to see another four years. Fragility. That is what the air of the last few days brings. All these precarious winds, shuffling branches and dismal skies begin to threaten the sunshine. Bring an ill-boding tone, a woeful wail. A thicker shirt. Flannel pajamas. Adjustments are made to tolerate the reality, to make it comfortable for us to live. Physical adjustments. Mental adjustments. Illusions in our lives exist in the successful alterations made to mask the unsaid truths shared on a hotline at 3 in the morning or festering in our heart's well of loneliness. Fragility showed on your face that night. That's what destroyed me, but there was something even more. More delicate, more tragic.

When humans are suffering from a terminal disease, they consciously know death is imminent. But you? When you exhibited all the textbook signs of dying, did you know what was happening? I don't know, but I believe you were completely unaware. You were searching for answers, you were listening to the disease, trying to figure it out and finally you looked at me. You looked at me for the answer, for relief, for a cure. Or at least to explain it. You put your fragility in my hands and a few hours later I ... I ... let you go. I'm beginning to concede how powerless I am, how uncertain are the days.

November 15

Avila Beach. Celebrating Melissa's birthday tonight when I received a text that Camille, one of my former students, died yesterday morning in a multi-car, fog-induced accident. 20 years old. A bustle of self-propelled, self-determined, resourceful energy. A blossoming force of prodigious intelligence, insight, and compassion. A cheerleading rebel. Taught her for two years. She adopted me, like students do with teachers, coming into my classroom every day at 2:25 to talk, laugh, bitch, cry. 20 years old. I've been holding onto my streak of no-tears since Kuma's death, thinking my surrender on October 4th an anomaly, even during this pandemic, and a year of incredible loss, but Camille's death, I believe, has permanently torn down my immunity bulwark and crossed the threshold of my empathy. It rattles my senses. It disfigures my thoughts. My soul is drowning in tears.

Starting to equate death's impact, regarding the degree of my visceral reaction, to the random slaughter of innocence, the unexpected nature of its appearance, and the victim's proximity to my present life. Mocking my diminished but somewhat reliable memory of what is and what was, I clearly can see this young woman laughing, self-conscious, feigning "I'm good" to a life unfairly framed in instability. I can hear her laughing, as vivid as I can see my Kuma Bear, and I am shaken beyond measure. Every death includes our own, but some leave us smaller and more unsettled than we were yesterday.

November 18

The current temperature evokes melancholia. I've been conditioned to feel sadness based on the weather and the school calendar. And so, we are getting to THE END OF THE YEAR! Leaves are down! Colors are dark. The end of . . . I spontaneously teared up for you today. Triggered by Nature once again. It was preceded by a litany of those people that have died this year, especially Camille, and then it ended with you. Kit arrives in less than a month. Just call me Judas. Brutus. Scottus.

November 30

Exactly one year ago my journal documents how life was teeming with holiday brunch, Trivial Pursuit, family movies, and how Kuma's surgery to remove his benign tumor went great. All upbeat and full speed ahead! Erasing all doubts, bathing in optimism, like killing one pesky cockroach in the kitchen has exterminated all. The enemy is vanquished; the battle is won!

The Blue Leash

But I didn't write again until Dec. 6th at four o'clock when Kuma's lymphoma knocked on our door with scythe in hand. From that point on, a pall hung over us all, a constant vigil accompanied his symptoms and decline. Every day I walk to relive that pain. Only to resuscitate and remember. To cherish a blessed time never to be repeated. Ever.

Growing up in Connecticut, I remember seeing women from all different nationalities – Italian, Polish, Portuguese – signaling the death of a family member by wearing some form of black. Some widows wore black for six months or a year; others for the rest of their lives. Black lace veils, black dresses or black armbands symbolizing their state of mourning to the community. To honor the dead, to share their loss, to allow others to share in their pain and empathize, thereby giving solace to their grief.

I guess the blue leash became my unofficial black veil. My pain to share, my memories to bear, and very, very slowly, my grief sullenly recedes. My walks in solitude with Kuma's leash traced my love and loss, and has served as a learned appreciation for the neighborhood – the trees, the houses, the people and the other dogs – and my life. Gratitude precedes my steps now for having had such a meaningful connection.

Scott D. DoVale

December 7, 2020

One year ago I videoed you at the beginning of our favorite walk. Knowing you had cancer but not knowing how soon you would depart. One minute and twenty-six seconds that I've watched for 359 days in a row. The enchanting tail, the bobbing head, eight feet in front, pace plowing ahead, peeing on the black twig, smelling the neighbor's petunias. I pull your leash to stop and say I love you. You look up at me, then look away and it's over.

These past two weeks I'm on a pilgrimage of our circuitous routes, our "greatest hits," around the neighborhood. Today the darkness of the streets indirectly embellishes my parade, my tribute. A tone more Covid-19 than post-Kuma these days. Gratitude grows as pain withers, smiles form instead of tears. Springtime in December. I still cry on a dime, though, whenever your name is evoked, knowing I will never see you again. Everything has its own time. One week from now, my fear of letting go will be severely tested. Final exam-ed. But we'll see . . . been studying for this one all year.

December 11

Starting my walk tonight looking at the pictures we took from your last three days on Earth, culminating with the last shot of us before you left. It's two days shy of you being gone for one year, but my tears still poured out from your absence. Your pure innocence. Your spirit. Your willingness

The Blue Leash

to be there for me, for 11 ½ years, filling our family, and myself, with unending affection, laughter and happiness. Pure heart. Impossible to thank you enough.

Tiffany, your first babysitter, wrote to say she was thinking of you this week. She recalled tending to your anxiety-induced insomnia, only weeks after your arrival, while the family vacationed in New England. How your persona requested space and distance, which bewildered her expectations, unsure if it was personal. We talked about how you always needed alone time, but when you chose to be present, you were present. No tomorrow or yesterday. No grudges or expectations. No apologies.

She also read President-elect Biden's book recently about his son's death and shared this one quote with me – "Every day you cry. Everything reminds you of something about them. Then one day you think of something about them and you smile. That's when you know you've turned the corner." I JUST WROTE THAT 4 DAYS AGO. Don't think I've turned the corner, though. To me, it's like asking someone, "When do you know you're an adult?" The answer lives inside each one of us.

(Midnight) Speaking of turning the corner, your breeder just texted me this minute. Our new baby Shiba, the pup we requested back in August and due this week, Kit, is a no-show. The breeder forgot to email us back in November, but the litter only produced three female Shibas. The message was disappointing but well-received. I will not push or force a different result. I will be patient. Just like you taught me. The universe has spoken. For now.

December 13

Kuma Bear Do Vale. If he were a human, he would be 5' 10", but everyone would assume he was over six feet. Red sesame hair, chiseled chin, beefy torso but strong, solid. Not like Deniro's Jake LaMotta. More like Kristofer Jivju's Tormand in *Game of Thrones*. Probably ends up being a college history professor. Marries in his thirties, making sure he's financially secure. In bars, he shoots a mean game of pool, drinks Maker's Mark Old-fashions, or Cadillac Margaritas. When he speculates about political cults, world injustices, political corruptions, and the demise of truth, no one interrupts. Drunk challenges elicit his Dirty Harry stare and the first punch, unflinchingly. He'd order a drink for the woman at the end of the bar. People would recognize his gentle exterior and warrior spirit. Try to emulate his speech and his walk.

He would not choose to hang out with me, unless I needed him. In fact, he walks with no one. Like Batman. Like the superhero living a double life at his own cost. But I would choose him like I did in this life. I would insist on being his partner in crime. His George Milton, his Lou Costello, his Dean Moriarty. I believe it was Mark Twain who said, "To get the full value of joy you must

The Blue Leash

have someone to divide it with." Yes, I still have Melissa, Kate and Max, but that's how it always felt, and I would love to share such joy with the human Kuma as well, even though he'd be a few inches taller than me.

"My life is not an apology, but a life. It is for itself and not for a spectacle. I much prefer that it should be of a lower strain, so it be genuine and equal, than that it should be glittering and unsteady."
– **Ralph Waldo Emerson**

The Blue Leash

Rolling Stone Issue 1336
February 3, 2020

Men live for all the wrong reasons. Men are taught to be strong warriors. To not show emotion. Work hard and emulate men of monetary wealth, men of wartime courage, ambitious men who strove to be the greatest, the best, regardless of what it takes to get there . . . whatever that means. The Puritan Ethic. The American Way.

Dogs, as well, receive the same misguided, narrow-minded versions of themselves. They are conditioned by a world that diminishes their interactions and communication down to the simplest of all existence. Sit. Beg. Go lay down. Go pee. Stop itching that! And without questioning the sources of these directions, as most humans, they play the roles handed down to them from past generations, trained to conform to human standards. To behave. To walk at a pace comfortable for humans. To not bark. To not dance. Everything that makes them unique is suppressed by fear as their innate and individual potentials are quickly squashed.

However, not every canine succumbs to the marching orders of the militaristic message in America that has left millions upon millions of men, women and dogs desperate, homeless, and shattered. Kuma, the Prince of the Chîsana Kamis, pranced on this Earth to a different Taiko drummer from 2008-2019. Although his departure seemed very sudden and premature to those he loved, as he mentioned in the following interview, he believed he achieved what Saisho, the Shiba Inu god, had intended for him to do – complete his "assignment." On December 14, 2019, at 11:44 pm, legendary Kuma Bear quickly succumbed to symptoms of lymphoma and was euthanized in Pasadena, California.

To honor his death, we thought it would be edifying to reprint Kuma's last interview with Rolling Stone in its entirety. As we look back, we are reminded of certain values Kuma emulated while he was here that are nearly extinct in American culture today. The interview was conducted by Jann W. on July 23rd, 2019, the 11- year anniversary of his cohabitation with the DoVale family.

The Blue Leash

Kuma "Bear" Do Vale:
The Interview

Nurtured by a graceful queue of oak trees on pointe with bras en couronne branches, paired with towering palms as havens for local parrots and crows, 100-year-old, face-lifted bungalows sit tucked under the gargantuan San Gabriel Mountains, numbering endlessly north of the 210 freeway in Pasadena, California. Unseen by most, except in the Best Neighborhoods in America issue of *Sunset Magazine*, lives a community peopled with not only JPL scientists, Cal Tech professors, and occasional Hollywood writers, directors, and film crew members, but one of the most culturally diverse canine communities this side of San Bernardino - German Shepherds, Scottish terriers, French poodles, Australian Shepherds, Siberian Huskies, Welsh Corgis - and quietly dwelling within this world of woofers, just blocks away from Eddie Van Halen's origin story, and recalling the Laurel Canyon heyday of Joni Mitchell and Stephen Stills, lives one of the wisest and furriest legends, Kuma Bear, a distinguished Japanese Shiba Inu and the Prince of the Chîsana Kamis.

Since his rise to prominence by his uncanny levitation over the Bungalow Heaven neighborhood in 2010, rather than cashing in on his decade-long fame, Kuma has lived an austere life. Our first interview with him, which was the first time he ever spoke to anyone, became our 3rd most popular issue of all time, only trailing the "Invasion of the Beatles" issue and "The Breakup of the Beatles." Now, in honoring his 11th anniversary, with his celebrity spurring the rise of the Shiba's popularity, a ubiquitous breed found on Instagram, Facebook and innumerable GIFs, we were compelled to visit him once again.

(Walking into Kuma's 103-year-old bungalow)

Very nice. Love the walnut trim, your bed, the sofa, collection of chew toys. Whoa! Mannequins. You have three mannequins, one with no head, and two dressed as Christmas elves surrounding your bed.

Part of Scott's classroom décor from last year. They're like having my own sentinels from the Nutcracker Suite. He does have an imaginative streak!

(Kuma leads me to the den, jumps up on the sofa. I sit in a chair opposite the sofa.)

It's been 10 years since you flew over the neighborhood, and yet so many people, especially the Baby Boomers and the Gen Zs, seem drawn to you. How might you explain your longer than 15 minutes of fame appeal?

I think people project much of their unsaid emotions on dogs. Have you seen how many dog movies and books there are these days? People and dogs have an extraordinary history of mutuality. Humans don't often acknowledge it, but they eventually form stronger bonds with their dogs than they do with some of their own family and friends. Not always but . . .

I've had that experience, too. I owned a dog once -

(mumbling growl) Whoa! Stop. A little too ethnocentric. You don't OWN a dog. You are assigned a dog. You are gifted a dog. *(Quickly starts nibbling his haunches).* Like the stars, the moon, a sunset over the Pacific.

Sorry. Let's talk about your journey. You were born in Oregon. Moved to California when you were eight weeks old. Pasadena. You gained a solid reputation throughout Bungalow Heaven, Lake Avenue and Old Town. In fact, according to a recent poll, your fan base here is second only to Jackie Robinson. Why do you think that is?

I guess when you live long enough, you get to know people. It took me a while to warm up to most of them. Very cautious when I was young. Protecting Scott's family was my main concern, but people gradually saw me for who I was. Loyal. Protective. Compassionate.

Up in Santa Barbara, you also have a large following, befriended by many of the locals. Lots of friends on State St.

Woof. True. We retreat there a few times a year, a little more when I was younger. And thinner! Great dog energy up there. People are less anxious, friendlier, and dogs are accepted everywhere. Stores, restaurants. But most of my friends hang out on State, East Beach, a few at the Funk Zone, a few at Motel 6.

Any thoughts on life in Southern California?

I'm in love with California. The weather, the beaches, the hotels. Even taking a walk I can go anywhere and just smell things for hours. *Festuca*? Incredible. Scent of a goddess! Anytime we walk I cannot pass a single patch of *Festuca*. Scott forces me to but if I was by myself... and I love the endless variety of dog breeds here as well. Barbets. Snickerdoodles?

But, overall, you've stayed relatively homebound. Has that been a conscious choice? Did you ever think about going up north to Carmel or spending time in the Bay Area?

I really didn't have a choice. I don't drive.

But Shibas are known to be "runners," right? My research says you guys are faster than a vaping greyhound.

But we're not long distance runners. That's over 300 miles. What's vaping?

Never mind.

We were born to run, so to speak. But that was only true for me when I was a pup. I did run away a few times but each time I came right back home.

And one of those times you famously *flew* back home?

Surprised the hell out of me! One minute I'm at a playdate licking a bone; the next minute I see the door open and BAM. My instinct was to run but after a few blocks, I got a bit confused. I know it's our nature, but why?

The Blue Leash

Life was real good right here. Anyway, I was running on empty, didn't know how to get back home. Lost the scent, walked a few blocks, and then all of a sudden, I'm floating. Then I'm flying over my neighborhood like a miniature google.earth.

How did you do it?

I'm not sure. I've brought it down to two things. Either my desire to go home might have lifted me off the ground, very *Wizard of Oz*-ish, or my concern for Scott. I was worried he would panic. Maybe call the police or have a heart attack. Either way, *thinking* about home somehow guided me home.

Unbelievable! You were featured in *Time*, *The New Yorker*, *Flying*, *Dogster*, and the cover of *Rolling Stone*. People stood outside your house with candles and dog treats for weeks. Kuma balloons were sold at the Rose Bowl, Halloween costumes of you wearing a cape became popular for several years. Your house was permanently placed on the annual Bungalow Heaven Tour!

That's right. We had a line of people around the block for months. I was afraid to go in the backyard to pee! It was not a blessing or a curse; it was just inconvenient.

Did you ever fly again?

Next question.

Kuma? Did you ever fly again?

(Kuma starts to clean himself.)

Ok, then, at the height of your popularity, why didn't you use your celebrity to expand your base, develop your brand, or sign a merchandising deal?

Wasn't in my heart.

Did you ever think of going the Marutaro route? He has 2.4 million Instagram followers. Any interest?

Marutaro was definitely not looking for fame; he just rolled over when it came. His assignment, Mr. Ono, no relation to Yoko, was inspired by the 2011 Tôhoku earthquake and tsunami. He wanted to lift up the spirits of the Japanese people, so he started posting pictures of Marutaro. Really cute pictures. Funny, sweet. Marutaro deserves his fame, and he definitely lived out his Shiba purpose but some of those poses? The costumes he had to wear? (*Shakes his head*) Then there was Doge. His real name was Kabosu. His assignment was an older woman, a teacher, very kind and loving, but she lost control of his image. Everybody was "Doge!" You couldn't see a Shiba Inu anywhere without someone yelling, "There's Doge! Doge!" Happens to me all the time. It's like when you keep hearing that #1 song on the radio too many times. It gets old real fast.

What about Bodhi?

Well, great gig if you want to be a menswear model. I'm not peeing on models, but I don't think I was put here to pose in front of a camera.

Doesn't everyone want to be famous?

Only in America.

When did you get this clear direction, this sense of self, or as Mr. Cameron writes, your purpose?

Let me just say this right now. *A Dog's Purpose* was a great book. In general, it really captures the essence of all dogs. Sure hope his premise is true! Anyway, my parents were very firm with me at an early age. They instilled in all of us, my brothers and sister, a code that our Shiba ancestors taught the early Samurai, by the time we were barely eight weeks old, one of selflessness, loyalty and honor. A few of my brothers didn't quite adapt to it, but it was everything I wanted. Great things to learn in puppyhood.

Is that a normal upbringing for dogs?

Most parents are teaching their pups not to poop on the carpet, be subservient, grateful, avoid chasing cars, don't bark too much. Except chihuahuas. They are raised to be yappers. (*Slight guffaw*) Shiba parents believe we are "different" than other dogs. Not stronger, not smarter but endowed with a spiritual purpose. Ok, maybe smarter. Historically, Shibas were marginalized for centuries. We had to fight stereotypes based on our cultural heritage, our good looks, our small stature, and our intelligence. We almost lost our breed at the turn of the 20th century because we were being crossbred to make other breeds stronger. That's why Shiba parents are more concerned in educating their pups and teaching them our history. They want to make sure their puppies achieve their destiny.

Would you say your upbringing has defined you?

It's guided me as far as keeping myself centered and helping Scott dig a little deeper. To recognize the details. Listen to others. Know silence. These are keys to living a conscious life.

I talked with Scott about your relationship. He said, "Kuma gave me back myself. He reached into my soul and connected me to all my former selves. The boy. The son. The drifting 20-year-old. He gave me structure and stability, but he also exposed me to things I might never have seen, and he made me laugh every single day. More than anyone else in my life."

(Kuma coughs) Do you want me to comment?

Is that how you see it?

Sure. Maybe I did all that but it's as much about him. He was open. He saw me for who I was. Any assignment, or any dog, has to be open – intellectually, emotionally – in order to have that type of growing experience. A teacher can have 30 students in a class - 10 absolutely love him; 10 think he's ok and 10 have no idea why they need to take the class. They're all listening to the same teacher but it's not the teacher; it's the student. So, yes, my relationship with Scott has been very rewarding but . . .

But?

No, I believe I've been true to my heritage. I brought him more clarity about his purpose, especially after Kate and Max went off to college. When they left Scott lost his

The Blue Leash

identity. He suffered anxiety, depression, drank a bit more but whenever he looked at me, I made sure he knew I was there for him and always will be until the end.

In the first RS interview, you were characterized as "feisty, independent, and arrogant." You admittedly nipped at least 10 people including Scott's mother, his brother and his best friend. Are you still that Shiba?

You've never been young? Maybe I was a bit too self-assured, confident, defensive. Definitely not arrogant. As I said before, I took my purpose seriously.

One of your closest friends, Winston, said you were the most well-read dog he's ever met, and he's been here a while. He was 19 years old when I talked to him and considering you're 11, in human years, that means . . .

Wait a minute. What if I were to say that you're what? 35? 36? "Hey, you've only lived 252 years! For every 52 human days" . . . I hate being constantly seen through a human lens. A privileged and myopic view dismissing my entire sense of being. It's so demeaning. It makes me want to . . . sorry, don't mean to piss on you. *(Coughs)* I'm just tired lately. Feel like I'm walking in wet kitty litter.

Sorry. I was trying to say you've accomplished quite a bit.

I never keep track of those things. Accomplishments? How fast can I run? How many flies I've eaten in one day? I look at things I'm grateful for, things people generally take for granted – waking up in the same bed together. Sharing breakfast. Greeting everyone at the door. Dinner. Being part of a family. That's my real accomplishment, to be part of the whole. I thought it was going to be a crate's life for me, but I was wrong. Life is so much more.

So, this is who you are. Not the biter or the independent runner but the family man?

Maybe I'm all of them at different times in different places. Emerson said, "To be yourself in a world that is constantly trying to make you something else is the greatest accomplishment." It's hard to be true to yourself. So much pressure to be someone else. Whenever I walk with Scott I see taller dogs, stronger dogs. Dogs with nicer collars, better fur, dogs sprinting and leaping after Frisbees. It all tugs at me, but as you get older, you learn to love yourself. The good and the bad. You understand context. What it means to be alive. At this point in my life, the only thing I care about is Scott and his family.

Seriously?

As soon as I hear his Jetta coming down the street, my tail has a mind of its own, waving like a rabid fan at her idol, and when he opens the door? I swoon. I start running in circles. I might jump on my hind legs. I don't even know what I'm going to do! And Mom! Kate! Max! It's like having your favorite bone while sticking your face out the car window and sniffing JLo's hoochie-coo all rolled into one.

The Blue Leash

JLo?

She's the orange Pomeranian three doors down. Leaves me pee notes on our bushes.

So, Scott is your true joy? And his family. Nothing else? Not even flying?

Yea, being with Scott. Sleeping with him and Mom. But whenever we walk together? Best.

I'm sure. Stuck in the house all day. You finally get some fresh air –

Yes, but . . . and this sounds strange but when I'm home I sleep quite a bit. I've never been one for laying around the house all day, but age right now is kicking my haunches. So, walking for me is a time for solitude, for purifying myself from everything else like having a Thoreau moment around the pond. But sharing solitude, being alone together, which sounds like an oxymoron but sharing time and space? Absolute doggie heaven.

Very introspective. Mindful. Not quite what I expected.

"When society is made up of men who know no interior solitude it can no longer be held together by love." Thomas Merton. Too many look outside for the answers, and they don't take the time to look inside. That's what's best about Scott. He's like a Shiba. Solitude is essential to our core, and walking with Scott is being with myself because we both thirst to maintain our interior life in an amoral and materialistic society.

I need a bit of that solitude myself. Thank you for that. *(Pause)* Is there a memorable time in your life? Anything stick out? Flying must be number one.

The day Scott saved my life.

Did you get hit by a car or something?

2016. I just came back from the dentist. They sedated me because my instinct is to bite people whenever they try to put their hand in my mouth.

***(Laughs)* Me, too! Sorry.**

I came home still feeling drowsy so I laid down on the couch. About an hour later, I'm having a hard time breathing. Couldn't even yodel for help. I started to lose consciousness when all of a sudden, I saw Scott fly out from his office. He yelled my name, started to check my breath. He stuffed a cookie in my mouth and when I didn't eat it, he knew something was wrong. Then he picked me up, and my head flopped down like a kettle bell on his shoulder. He lost it! He ran to his car, put me in the front seat, called the vet, yelled to his son, and sped to the vet like a coyote with his tail on fire. Next thing I know, I'm waking up in the operating room with some nurses smiling down at me. I thought I was going to meet Saisho.

If Scott was in the office, how did he know you were in trouble?

Whenever the mailman drops the mail through our mail slot, I usually scream and growl, start tearing up the mail, but when he didn't hear me attack it, he instinctively knew something was wrong. Very Shiba-like.

The Blue Leash

Nice connection.

As if he was my father. He knows me so well, more than I ever thought possible.

How does it feel to be that dependent? I mean when you're human, you eventually move away from your parents, which you did, but I mean . . . you know, you're not out there foraging for food. You have a bed, a couch, 2-3 meals a day, walks. Does that affect your self-esteem in any way?

What you're bringing up are the basic needs of humans and dogs. We're all dependent beings.

Yes, but if Scott doesn't provide you with food and shelter -

(Kuma's fur rises.) Why do you think Scott picks up my poop? Walks me, feeds me, strokes me? Why are there over 63 million dog owners in America?

I guess people like to have something to pet. Like plants or stuffed animals or blankies.

Really? That's what you think?

This isn't my wheelhouse. I've never sat down and thought about it.

Ever read Steinbeck's *Of Mice and Men*?

About 100 years ago. But I remember the story.

Lennie and George. George is physically small but street smart, knows how to get them jobs as itinerant farm workers. Gets the food. The shelter. Lennie's a big man, a strong worker but mentally challenged, can't take care of his basic needs.

In that scenario, you see Scott as George and yourself as Lennie. Minus the "mentally challenged" part, obviously.

Right, everyone assumes Lennie is the dependent one because he is limited in providing those basic needs for himself.

Isn't that right?

And because Lennie's limitations keep getting him and George in trouble, George is eventually forced to kill Lennie, to "euthanize" him, in order to save his own life.

But if Lennie kept getting George in trouble, why didn't George just leave him a long time ago? Like run away some night and let Lennie fend for himself?

But isn't leaving him the same as killing him? Why do you think George took care of Lennie for so long if he caused him so much trouble?

Well, at least he's not alone?

Bingo! Steinbeck was exposing how loneliness was detrimental to the other characters whereas Lennie and George were special. Lennie also looked up to George. He admired George, saw only the good in him. Like a younger brother who looks up to his older brother. What Lennie gave George was self-worth, identity and purpose. A belief in himself he never had before.

That's pretty good.

Without Lennie, George becomes like every other farm hand. Alone. *(Pause)* All I'm saying is Scott and I share

The Blue Leash

a similar relationship. We need each other. We are better because of each other.

Winston was right. Is that your favorite book?

I have two - *The Art of Racing in the Rain* and *Invisible Man*. The one by Ralph Ellison.

Favorite song?

"Who Let the Dogs Out?" *(Coughs "Bulldog shit!")* Just kidding. I would say "Brothers on a Hotel Bed." Death Cab. No, no!!! "What a Wonderful World" with Louis Armstrong. Final answer. The family always sings it on New Year's Eve. *(Pants a little, gets water)* Yeah. That's the one.

If you knew tomorrow was your last day . . . Vegas? In-N-Out? Motel 6?

These questions are *(coughs)* . . . I feel like this is the "last interview" interview. Like Jim Morrison or Janis Joplin might have felt before their demise. Ok, that's before my time, but it works!

Your last day?

I might not live forever, but if I'm pursuing my dream when I die, I'll be happy. Thoreau's idea about pursuing your dream and meeting with unexpected success? *(Pause. His eyes start to tear.)* I knew I had a good assignment; I just never knew I would feel *Ai*.

Ai?

Japanese for love. Never saw it coming.

Not on your radar?

Shibas are independent. We are taught to be loyal. We

don't operate on emotion. I love my parents but that's different. I love my heritage, my breed, but I also think age has forced me to see my life differently. More clearly. It isn't only having an assignment and doing my duty. From the time he wakes up until he comes to bed, I truly care about him.

Why do you think that is? You said your parents taught you –

Parents can only teach you so much. They want you to be safe. To protect you from harm. But I see dogs who have so much less. Every day when we walk, I smell pain. Some of it comes from their upbringing, their lack of purpose. But quite a bit of it comes from them not being seen by their family as anything but an object. An accessory. But Scott . . . ok, last quote. Scott is like Gatsby's smile - "It understood you just so far as you wanted to be understood, believed in you as you would like to believe in yourself."

I can't believe you remember all these quotes.

He taught *The Great Gatsby* 18 times.

Very impressive. Do you have any regrets? Have you accomplished your Chîsana Kami destiny?

I believe I always have more to give. I feel we are all here to plant seeds, seeds that may inspire spiritual growth and beauty. I know my "assignment" has been touched by my life, but he still has a few seeds that may blossom after I'm gone. I pray they serve him well.

The Blue Leash

Ok, I need to get this in. You started a support group for dogs. Want to talk about it?

Initially, I named it BLM – Beagles Lives Matter. Kate and Max weren't looking for a Shiba when they were looking for a dog. They wanted a beagle. Then here comes a Shiba. Perfect face, beautiful fur, yada, yada, yada. Raised in a caged community with only other Shibas, living a privileged life, yada, yada, yada.

I felt bad for beagles. They could easily have made Kate and Max happy. Any dog has the potential to make any human happy. As a Shiba, you get jaded. You don't realize you're seeing the world through a very narrow lens. You assume everyone is raised in a nurturing community with great parents and treated like their life matters. And that's not just Shibas. Smooth Fox Terriers won't even look at me. Tibetan Mastiffs? And now Corgis? There always seems to be certain breeds on the top which makes for a very populated bottom. After a year, I changed BLM to PLM – Pitbulls Lives Matter. No dogs have been more stigmatized, abused, abandoned and/or euthanized during my lifetime.

Why not DLM?

That's understood. Even strays know that! But unless someone else treats you like ... did you know Pitbulls were used as nannies to watch over babies in Europe? Steinbeck owned pitbulls. So did Helen Keller and Dr. Seuss. Always nurture over Nature. People need to stop judging by breed or color or age. Strays, rescues, physically challenged. We're all dogs! We all have the right to a good life. We all have the potential to love and be loved. So, right now there needs to be an awareness and a conscious shift on how people treat Pitbulls. Just love them! They'll be great. All they need is love.

You know you sound quite a bit like Scott.

Well, when you live with someone for 11 years, you tend to do that.

"Some souls leave behind a trail of light that is never forgotten"
– a mystic

The Blue Leash

December 14, 2020

To my Prince:

These fingers tremble. I've been anticipating this day since August, when the first day of retirement marked your absence. The weight of this moment burns down my aging face. Years of coming home to a wild-eyed fanatical Shiba, an unleashed fan club of one, my guardian angel prancing through every room, shadowing me, questioning me, listening, grumbling, begging, pushing me away, engaging me and sustaining me in an 11 ½ year drift of soon-to-be back stories. Now I, too, sit in the dark recesses of my office with labored breath, hiding from the inescapable and I, too, decelerate for my last 125 steps without you.

Swirling over rooftops, remote and alone, alone in Chagall's "Over the Town," viewing all that was and all that is now. Abandoned streets. Lonely lawns. Forlorn trees.

Scott D. DoVale

Picnic tables sitting unfulfilled. A fractured park. Strangers askew as the squirrels, crows, and Pasadena parrots perform less than yesterday. No one knowing how or why. Walking without an owner's manual or a game pamphlet of directions and rules. Who goes first? (You did). And yet? This epic mural entices us and shapes us with every color, garnished with sound, smell and taste, permeating hope within all living and non-living things. The incessant movement of life – walking, running, darting, swaying, bouncing, rolling, circling, hugging, kissing – each contributing a shade of illusion to the mysterious masterpiece, morphing a new dimension, carving a new path, offering happiness and security, fun and freedom, creating more and more distractions and discrepancies. Alternative facts. Cover-up tattoos. But we know what was and what is now because we lived it.

One year has passed. These Kuma-less mornings bear no magic. I stir and stumble. A listless life of coffee, workouts, emails, retired people chores, buying a quart of this to paint that, a quick Covid-19 browse for a book destined for a log-jammed shelf. Maybe nap for 30. But around noon I leave the monotonous world behind to feast on pixelated glimmers, retracing our abbreviated journey, leading me to strike out on this broken telegraph until night. Revisiting pavement patterns in the park, pausing at the entrance boulders, touching brown bushes, smelling forgotten ferns, watching other people's dogs, bemoaning my loss, pouting

The Blue Leash

my protest to heaven. Wading through gray matter, seeking posttraumatic growth as I stitch threads of lost time together with regret, flashbacks with smiles, holidays with tears while wingless vultures of human righteousness circle my heart. A daily journey once around the sun, back where I started from and waiting for tomorrow.

Meanwhile, your home companions attempt to raise our spirits auditioning for your vacated starring role. Theo mimics your flop, shoots his feline rigor mortis paws in the air, begs for belly rubs and occasionally sleeps on the enshrined Kuma bed. Twice I found him sitting in your crate, possibly contemplating a species conversion. Kimba, Theo's antagonist, dares to sleep on our bed during the day, laps water from the sacred bowl and marches boastfully around the house carrying your blue bone in his mouth as if he just conquered Rome. Olympia, however, rescued almost three years ago, continues to prefer solitary confinement in her crate. In other words, she's still the same Shiba recluse, content being away from the drama, a shrewd demeanor paralleling my own impulse for self-preservation.

As a teenager, I cultivated a similar attitude, isolating myself from emotional pain, lopping off personal relationships like dead branches. A defense mechanism honed for decades to stay in control, not let anyone dictate my life. I'm drawn back to Hester in *The Scarlet Letter*, as she isolates herself from the Puritans by living outside the community while being ostracized by them for being a sinner. Just like Hester and Olympia, I never turned around. Never thought about what ifs. Just kept moving on. Until December 14, 2019. Your death jarred me, unearthing a blind spot ignored for too many years. The depth of my pain was so new, so dark and yet, as I tried to share it, takers were few. It reminded me of how callous I have been to friends in need throughout the years. How insensitive I was to not see beyond my own pain to help theirs. So, failing to be heard in time of need felt like karmic payback, a much-needed wake-up call from the universe to repent.

However, generally speaking, mourning a dog's death in a human world sounds oxymoronic and a waste of time. Like pearls before swine. Incongruous. Like rawhide bones before cats. In my daily life, I became silent, unable to share my grief any further, anticipating the derision, the questioning looks, and the therapist referrals. On Facebook and Instagram, I see it takes a click to mourn, maybe 5 teary-faced emojis, and then everyone's back to today's GIFs and LOLs. I understand. There are also Covid victims and BLM victims; there are deaths of family members and friends, personal tragedies and losses, random murders, hate crimes, school shootings, mass murders, and I completely understand. *TIME MARCHES ON!* Life is full of death – victims and survivors. *DON'T BE LIKE LOT'S WIFE!* Life is fragile and unpredictable. *AND TIME MARCHES ON!* But this is my life . . .

The Blue Leash

"For I have known them all already, known them all —
Have known the evenings, mornings, afternoons,
I have measured out my life with coffee spoons;
I know the voices dying with a dying fall
Beneath the music from a farther room.
So how should I presume?"
- The Love Song of J. Alfred Prufrock, T. S. Eliot

On earth, we are destined to know pain and suffering, to feel hopeless and lost, but to experience mutuality and loyalty, to share solitude and stability? It was a gift. You offered me the freedom to be unconditionally me. You exposed me to a world I had shunned, thinking it frivolous, fictitious and delusional. For many years I sat in Plato's cave until you showed me the fire and the shadows. Grateful for the conversations, for the companionship, for your lessons on simplicity and selfless love. For your patience. To quote John, Mom's hair stylist, after adopting his first puppy several months ago, "I never knew I could love so deeply."

Tomorrow I rise without a familiar route. Just a blue leash and a journal. Not sure if I continue my walks or invent something new, like giving out doggie treats at the park in your honor or starting a posthumous Instagram account prophesizing your second coming! Whatever I choose to do, I will be thinking of you. My internal karaoke will be searching for the perpetual swan song, the last hurrah anthem. George Fenton's cliff scene music in *The Crucible*. Gus' eulogy for Hazel Grace. Or Rickie Lee Jones singing *Company*:

> *"I'll see you in another life now, baby*
> *I'll free you in my dreams*
> *But when I reach across the galaxy*
> *I will miss your company."*

About a month after you died, I went to dinner with your first babysitters, and my best friends, Tiffany and Liz. We were catching up and sharing monumental moments from the past year. One of them painted an impressionistic tableau of sipping champagne on Bastille Day under the glowing Eiffel Tower. The other alluded to our mutual love for Thoreau and Nature, recalling her sublime moment atop Half Dome in Yosemite, and more recently watching dolphins surround her boat as she sailed the Pacific out to Catalina. When they were done, their eyes looked to me, and I did not flinch.

It was late July, 2019, a Sunday morning at the Blue Sands Inn. We were sitting by the pool, waiting for the others to go to brunch. The sun warming our tired faces, the sky blew bluer at us deeper than love itself. I had on my Packers shirt, black jeans, nursing a Knob Creek headache. You were nestled next to me, exhausted from travel, your head lounging on my lap like a sea lion on his favorite rock.

The Blue Leash

My arm felt the import, softly hugging your familiarity, your trust and infinite understanding. Your infinite love. This was you and me. Me and you. Feeling infinite.

These days I'm living life in braille but aware of how fortunate we were this time around. I lived you, breathed you, held you, walked you. For my next life, I only wish for warm breezes, endless beaches, cool oceans, blue silence, the divine, the rolling hills leading up to St. Mary's Church, my ultimate playlist and your infinite presence. Your burly body next to mine, floating around on a plush Helix cloud, keeping each other company as we wait for the rest of the family. I pray eternal life dismantles me down to my essence, strips me of anxiety and fear, ego and lust, anger and hate, vanity and pride, and grants me my angel once again, my Chîsana Kami, to live my days in peace. Until then, my love and gratitude will be here until my last breath.
Thank you, Kuma Bear.
You were the One.

Scott D. DoVale

Acknowledgements

I am deeply grateful for the following people who supported me during this process. To Dawn Raffel, for her nurturing editorial voice, guidance and the title; Jane Osick, for her literary wisdom, honesty and friendship; Darryl Oliver, for his direction and encouragement, and Elysia Clapin, for her book design and patience. A special thank you to Amy Wang, for her artistic talent and constant inspiration. I am also grateful for friends who are extraordinary readers – Paula, Amy, Tiff, Pam and my son, Max. Finally, this book does not exist without my wife, Melissa, for believing in me these past thirty years.

About the Author

Scott DoVale grew up in Danbury, Connecticut. In 1976, he graduated from the Culinary Institute of America and lived in kitchens for the next twenty-four years. He wrote his first play, *Voices in the Dark*, in 1991, which was performed in Hollywood and Santa Monica, and awarded a grant from the Los Angeles Dept. of Cultural Affairs. He returned to college at forty, taught American literature in high school for 19 years, and while earning his Masters in Creative Writing at Cal State Northridge, he wrote his second play, *Fascinum Wireless*. He currently lives in Pasadena, California and writing his second book, *Heartless*.

www.ingramcontent.com/pod-product-compliance
Lightning Source LLC
Chambersburg PA
CBHW070139100426
42743CB00013B/2757